Cooking for Two

With the Micheff Sisters

A Vegan Vegetarian Cookbook

Also by the Micheff sisters
Cooking With the Micheff Sisters
Cooking Entrees With the Micheff Sisters

3ABN BOOKS is dedicated to bringing you the best in published materials consistent with the mission of Three Angels Broadcasting Network. Our goal is to uplift Jesus Christ through books, audio, and video materials by our family of 3ABN presenters. Our in-depth Bible study guides, devotionals, biographies, and lifestyle materials promote whole person health and the mending of broken people. For more information, call 618-627-4651 or visit 3ABN's Web site: www.3ABN.org

Designed by Michelle C. Petz
Front cover and interior recipe photos by Mark Mosrie

Unless otherwise noted all Bible verses are from the NKJV Bible version.

Additional copies of this book are available from two locations:
3ABN: Call 1-800-752-3226 or visit online at www.3ABN.org
Adventist Book Centers: Call toll-free 1-800-765-6955 or visit online at
AdventistBookCenter.com

Library of Congress Cataloging-in-Publication Data

Johnson, Linda Micheff, 1951-
Cooking for two with the Micheff sisters : a vegan vegetarian cookbook / Micheff sisters.
p. cm.
Includes index.
ISBN-13: 978-0-8163-2258-9 (pbk.)
ISBN-10: 0-8163-2258-9 (pbk.)
1. Vegan cookery. 2. Vegetarian cookery. 3. Cookery for two.
I. Walsh, Brenda Micheff, 1953- II. Sanner, Cinda Micheff, 1955- III. Title.

TX837.J5425 2008
641.5'636—dc22
2007047155

08 09 10 11 12 • 5 4 3 2 1

Cooking for Two
With the Micheff Sisters

A Vegan Vegetarian Cookbook

3ABN BOOKS

P.O. Box 220, West Frankfort, Illinois
www.3ABN.org

Pacific Press® Publishing Association
Nampa, Idaho
Oshawa, Ontario, Canada
www.pacificpress.com

Foreword

It seems like only yesterday when my little girls were standing on their stools by my side helping me prepare our family meals. They would watch how I did things and then would try to imitate me. As I looked down at my happy, precious girls mixing ingredients in their very own bowls, I never dreamed that God would use them in such a mighty way to encourage others to eat healthfully.

When I was growing up, I never had the opportunity to learn how to cook. More importantly, I didn't have a mom who was willing to patiently teach me. I only share this because so many times wives and mothers use this excuse for their unwillingness to even try to prepare healthy meals for their families. I believe in the promise in Philippians 4:13, "I can do all things through Christ who strengthens me." It doesn't matter how lacking we are in culinary skills, our heavenly Father sees our need and will help us if we ask Him. Jesus says in Philippians 4:19 that "God shall supply all your need . . ." and I have found that His promises are true and reliable.

God has been so patient with me.

When I first began making meals, I had many failures before learning to make food that my family really enjoyed eating! But always my precious Jesus would encourage me. I held on to His promises and He not only helped me learn to make delicious meals but blessed my children in knowing how to cook as well!

God gave me confidence and helped me to teach my children the joy of cooking. He will help you too. Spending time in the kitchen with my girls, as well as with my sons, has not only given us cherished memories but has enriched our lives spiritually as well. God always blesses the time we spend with our children. My heart is filled with joy as I see God using each one of them to be a blessing to others.

Now when I prepare meals, it is mostly just for Dad and me, except for our drop-in guests and friends. Of course, that's no problem at all since I still know how to add more water and seasonings to the soup! I am especially excited about this new cookbook, *Cooking for Two With the Micheff Sisters.* Now my girls are teaching me new recipes! I'm sure you will enjoy them too. As you strive to have a healthier life, may you experience the blessing in 3 John 2, "Beloved, I pray that you may prosper in all things and be in health, just as your soul prospers."

Bernice Micheff
Mother of Linda, Brenda, and Cinda

Tribute

We dedicate *Cooking for Two With the Micheff Sisters* to our precious husbands, Jim, Tim, and Joel. They have faithfully stood by us in every aspect of our ministry. We couldn't do what we do without them and their loving support.

Every time we prepare a cookbook to share with others, we have counted on our husbands to be our taste testers. Although they didn't always love everything we created, an encouraging look from them would inspire us to keep on trying. Once they gave the dish their thumbs-up, we knew it was definitely a recipe we could share! Most importantly, they have not only been our taste testers but also our prayer partners. Their loving prayers and encouragement have been a great source of earthly strength for us as we work in children's ministries, present seminars, speak, tape cooking programs, or perform whatever task God has for us to do. We truly thank God for giving us such special husbands.

Jim, Tim, and Joel, we want you to know that we are so blessed to have you for our companions on this journey to eternity. We truly look forward to spending not only the rest of our lives together here on earth, but we are excited about living forever with you in heaven.

We love you with all our hearts,
Linda, Brenda, and Cinda.

Acknowledgments

We would like to express our heartfelt thanks to all those who helped make
Cooking for Two With the Micheff Sisters possible.

We appreciate Three Angels Broadcasting Network and their worldwide ministry in promoting
Bible truths and the health message. We are thankful to 3ABN for giving us the opportunity
to share with others the abundant lifestyle that God offers.

We want to thank our precious parents for their unfailing love, patience, listening ears,
and constant prayers, and for always being there for us. Thank you, Mom, for teaching us the joy
of cooking when we were young children and encouraging us to be ourselves. Today, we credit our
individual cooking styles to you. But most of all, thank you both for making Jesus the center of our home
and inspiring us to share God's love with others. Mom and Dad, we love you with all our hearts!

We also want to thank Pacific Press®, our publisher, for their many hours of hard work to make this
cookbook possible: Russ Holt for encouraging us to create the recipes (without him, this book would not
have been written!); Tim Lale for support, direction, and gentle reminders to meet our deadline; Aileen
Andres Sox for her many hours editing recipes; and last but not least, Michelle Petz
for creating yet another beautiful cookbook design and cover!

Most of all we want to thank our awesome God for His many blessings and unconditional love
for each one of us. We love You, Jesus, and we are looking forward to spending eternity with You!

Table of Contents

Introduction 8

Substitutions 9

Breakfast & Breads 11

Salads & Sandwiches 33

Soups & Stews 53

Entrées & Side Dishes 75

Fast & Easy 97

Desserts 115

Resources 138

Time-saving Tips 140

Measurements & Equivalents 142

Index 143

Introduction

It seems like only yesterday, we were small children creating mud pies filled with berries from our mulberry tree. We spent hours trying to perfect our work to make it look delicious. Our creations were garnished with dandelions, pretty weeds, and anything else we could find outdoors that looked interesting. As she monitored our play, Mom would sometimes tell us that some plants were harmful and needed to be left alone. Proudly we presented our finished creations to Daddy who would wrinkle up his nose and make a hideous face. Of course, this would send us into fits of laughter and inspire us to make something even more enticing! As we look back at our childhood, it amazes us to realize that even in our playtime, God was preparing us for ministry.

Mom's wisdom of yesterday still holds true in our real preparation of foods. There are still harmful things to leave out of foods. High fat, sodium, and sugar are not good for our bodies. These foods contribute to heart disease, cancer, high blood pressure, and a host of other illnesses. Yes, they taste good, but it is not worth the damage it causes to our bodies. All too soon our bodies start to deteriorate and can no longer fight these poisons.

More and more we see the wisdom in eating more fruits, vegetables, grains, and nuts. God made so many wonderful foods that not only give vitality and strength but bless us emotionally and spiritually as well. We realize eating healthfully is a daily learning process. However, we don't want to become so consumed with diet that it becomes our religion.

Jesus wants us to live a balanced life like He did while living on this earth. Unless we have good health, we won't have the energy to go to the ends of the earth to share the good news of salvation and Christ's soon coming, as we have been commissioned to do. Truly, we have found that there is no greater joy than to share Jesus!

We believe our cookbooks are only a stepping-stone to better health, and we have tried to create recipes that are fast and easy to prepare. *Cooking for Two With the Micheff Sisters* was inspired by a woman at a Kansas-Nebraska camp meeting who wanted a cookbook that would meet her and her husband's needs. God used Bonnie Laing, whom we affectionately call "Sister Binda," to put a spark in us to meet this need. We all felt we had too much to do to attempt another cookbook this year—much less one that is all small recipes! But like everything else, we took this project before the Lord and felt impressed to accept the challenge. And here it is! As we keep progressing in our efforts to have better health, we will be one step closer to the abundant life God has in store for us!

With God's richest blessings,
Linda, Brenda, and Cinda
the Micheff sisters

Substitutions

MILK SUBSTITUTES

Soy Good is a vegan soymilk by Dressler's, and one of our favorites. There are two kinds: plain and simple, which is good for soups and gravies, and the regular vanilla Soy Good, which has a green label and is good for anything that requires a sweeter taste. For more information, check our resource page.

Better Than Milk original flavor is great to cook with and is great for cold cereals. The vanilla flavor is good for cookies, cakes, and baked goods.

Nondairy whipped topping is a milk-free item that can be found in most of your local grocery stores. If the grocery store does not offer this product, be sure and ask them to carry it.

NATURAL SWEETENERS

Florida Crystals is milled sugarcane and can be used as white sugar one cup for one cup. It is our choice for many recipes, but especially those that need to be light in color.

Pure maple syrup is inexpensive if purchased at large membership stores. Use in muffins, breads, cookies, pancakes, fruit smoothies, and desserts.

Frozen fruit juices are all-natural sweeteners. Just be sure the label says 100 percent juice. Use in fruit sauces, pies, smoothies, and baked goods.

Sucanat by Wholesome Foods is organic evaporated sugarcane juice with blackstrap molasses added to it. It replaces brown and white sugar one for one.

TOFU

Tofu is an excellent source of protein and contains no cholesterol. It also is an inexpensive substitute for meat, fish, poultry, and cheese.

Silken Tofu is a soybean product with a silky smooth texture. It's great for cheesecakes, pies, puddings, and salad dressings.

Water-packed tofu comes in soft, firm, or extra-firm. It has to be refrigerated and has a shorter expiration date. Water-packed tofu has a firmer, spongier texture, and it is great for things like mock scrambled eggs. It can be crumbled and will hold its shape so it is very useful in all kinds of recipes. It can be blended until smooth or sliced or baked or boiled—the ideas are endless. It is a wonderful product.

Mori-Nu Tofu does not have to be refrigerated until opened and has a long shelf life. Mori-Nu is great for making entrees, desserts, salads, salad dressings, dips, soups, mock egg salad, and many other dishes.

Mori-Nu Mates, in lemon and vanilla flavors, can be found in the health food section of large grocery stores. This product can also be purchased through Country Life Natural Foods.

OTHER PRODUCTS

Tofutti Sour Supreme is our favorite sour cream substitute. It looks and tastes close to dairy sour cream but is milk and butterfat free. It contains no cholesterol. This product can be found nationally in most health food stores and select supermarkets. Substitute this product in any recipe that calls for sour cream.

Tofutti Better Than Cream Cheese is a great substitute for cream cheese. It is milk and butterfat free and contains no cholesterol. It is great for making entrées, desserts, or just used as a spread for bagels.

Grapeseed Oil Vegenaise and Original Vegenaise, both by Follow Your Heart, are great mayonnaise replacements. Grapeseed oil is an excellent natural source of vitamin E and essential fatty acids necessary for normal cell metabolism and maintenance. Vegenaise is found only in the refrigerated sections of your grocery stores.

Bragg Liquid Aminos is an unfermented soy sauce replacement. It can be used in entrées, Oriental foods, to marinate gravies, and in any recipe that calls for soy sauce.

Brewer's yeast flakes are made of nutritional yeast, which is one of the most perfect foods known. It is a powerful health source of B vitamins, amino acids, proteins, minerals, enzymes, and nucleic acids. This premium yeast is grown on sugar beets, which are known to absorb nutrients from the soil faster than almost any other crop. As a result, this yeast is exceptionally rich in selenium, chromium, potassium, copper, manganese, iron, zinc, and other factors natural to yeast. It is also gluten free. This yeast can be used as a breading, in entrées, or sprinkled on top of foods like popcorn, tofu scrambled eggs, and so forth.

Carob chips are a great alternative to chocolate chips. Some carob chips have dairy and lots of sweeteners in them, so look for the vegan ones sweetened with barley malt. These can be found in your local co-ops, health food stores, or larger grocery stores.

Rumford's Baking Powder is an aluminum-free baking powder.

Egg replacer can be found in larger grocery stores. Cornstarch can be used as an egg replacer also.

Soy margarine may be found in your local grocery store. Find a brand that is vegan, non-hydrogenated and has no trans fats and no cholesterol.

Pecan meal is simply pecans that have been ground into a fine meal. This product can usually be found in your local grocery store or purchased at larger grocery stores. To make your own, just put the pecans in the blender and blend until it is the right consistency. Walnuts can be substituted in any of our recipes that call for pecans.

Vege-Sal is a seasoned salt that is available in the health food section of most grocery stores.

Breakfast & Breads

Cinnamon &
Raisin Bread
p. 30

Maple Almond
Granola
p. 27

Picante Tofu
Scramble
p. 25

Honey Corn Bread
Muffins
p. 29

Grandma's
Breakfast Hash
p. 24

Sweet Potato
Waffles
p. 15

Multigrain Waffles

1 cup whole wheat pastry flour

1 tablespoon baking powder

1/2 cup quick or old-fashioned oats

1/4 teaspoon salt

2 tablespoons ground flaxseed

1/2 cup applesauce

1/2 cup pure maple syrup

1 1/4 to 1 1/2 cups soymilk

Combine all dry ingredients in a large bowl. Mix well. Add applesauce, pure maple syrup, and enough soymilk to reach a consistency slightly thicker than pancake batter. Mix well by hand. Batter can be a little lumpy. Pour into a preheated waffle iron and cook 3 to 4 minutes or until golden brown. Serve hot.

These fluffy, moist waffles are wonderful with a variety of toppings, such as warm applesauce or one of your favorite fruits. If you like something more traditional, pure maple syrup is delicious too! I like to double this batch so I have extras to store in the freezer. All you have to do is pop them in the toaster and in minutes they are ready to eat! —Brenda

Yield: 4 waffles

(Per waffle) Calories: 308   Total Fat: 3.5g   Saturated Fat: 0.4g   Sodium: 295.0mg   Carbohydrates: 62.7mg   Fiber: 6.7g   Protein: 6.2g

Sweet Potato Waffles

In a large bowl, mix together all dry ingredients. Then add sweet potatoes, oil, syrup, and pure vanilla extract. Mix well. Slowly add soymilk until the consistency is slightly thicker than pancake batter. Use additional soymilk as needed. (Moisture content of batter varies due to the moisture content of the mashed sweet potatoes.) Pour 1 cup batter into a hot waffle iron and bake until steam stops escaping: 3 to 4 minutes depending on your individual waffle iron. Waffles should be golden, slightly crispy on the outside and tender and moist on the inside. Serve hot.

These waffles have the flavor of pumpkin pie with a bread texture. I love to add raisins or crushed pineapple for variety. If you don't like nuts, just leave them out. They are good just as they come out of the waffle iron. I suggest adding some pure maple syrup! Mmm, mmm, good! Make extra because these waffles freeze well for 2 to 3 months. When you are ready to eat, just pop them in your toaster! Now that is what I call a fast and easy breakfast! —Brenda

1 1/4 cups whole wheat pastry flour

2 teaspoons baking powder

1/2 teaspoon salt

1 teaspoon ground cinnamon

1/2 teaspoon ground ginger

1/4 teaspoon ground nutmeg

1/8 teaspoon ground cloves

1/2 cup pecan pieces

1 cup cooked and mashed sweet potatoes

1/4 cup canola oil

1/3 cup pure maple syrup

1 teaspoon pure vanilla extract

2 cups soymilk (more as needed)

Yield: 4 waffles

(Per waffle) Calories: 492   Total Fat: 24.3g   Saturated Fat: 2.1g   Sodium: 586.1mg   Total Carbohydrates: 63.5mg   Fiber: 8.2g   Protein: 7.4g

Apple Oat Waffles

1 cup whole wheat flour

1/2 cup quick rolled oats

1/4 cup cornmeal

1 teaspoon baking powder

1 cup grated fresh apple

1/4 teaspoon sea salt

1 1/4 cups soymilk

1 teaspoon pure vanilla
extract

1 tablespoon pure virgin
coconut oil

2 tablespoons pure maple
syrup

Mix all dry ingredients together. Make a well in the middle of dry ingredients, and add the rest of the ingredients. Gently mix together until smooth. (The batter will thicken the longer it sits. Add additional soymilk as needed.) Spray a hot waffle iron with nonstick cooking spray. Add approximately 1/2 cup batter and spread to the edges of the waffle iron. Bake 3 to 5 minutes until golden brown. Serve with peanut butter and hot applesauce. Garnish with fresh strawberries.

My friend Jan Lanaville cannot have anything with gluten in it. So I changed this recipe, using 1 1/4 cups brown rice flour in place of the whole wheat flour and oats. Jan loved the waffles and asked for the recipe so she could make them at home. These can be made ahead of time and frozen, then heated in the toaster. But they are best served fresh and hot. So try a batch and enjoy!
—Linda

Yield: 3 6-inch waffles

(Per waffle) Calories: 358   Total Fat: 8.0g   Saturated Fat: 4.7g   Sodium: 350.2mg   Total Carbohydrates: 65.0mg   Fiber: 7.4g   Protein: 9.8g

Pumpkin Pecan Pancakes

In a small mixing bowl, whisk together all dry ingredients. Mix well. Make a well in the center of dry ingredients. Add all liquid ingredients including pumpkin. Stir until well blended. Spray griddle or frying pan with nonstick cooking spray and heat to medium. (If cooking surface is too hot, pancakes will burn.) Pour 1/4 cup batter for each pancake. Wait until pancake starts to bubble and becomes firm, then flip. Pancake is done when the center springs back slightly when touched with a finger. Pancakes will be golden, soft, light, and fluffy. Serve with pure maple syrup.

These pancakes are absolutely melt-in-your-mouth wonderful for breakfast or a perfect choice for a fancy brunch! Sometimes I serve them with my home-canned applesauce. I do want to warn you, however, that they sometimes disappear before I can actually get them to the table! An added bonus—the delicious aroma of vanilla and cinnamon! —Brenda

3/4 cup whole wheat pastry flour

1 teaspoon baking powder

1/4 teaspoon baking soda

1/2 teaspoon cinnamon

1/8 teaspoon ground ginger

Pinch cloves

1 teaspoon salt

1/4 cup chopped pecans

1 tablespoon cornstarch

1/2 cup pure maple syrup

3/4 cup soymilk

1/2 teaspoon pure vanilla extract

1/2 cup canned pumpkin

Yield: 8 4-inch pancakes

(Per pancake) Calories: 132 Total Fat: 2.9g Saturated Fat: 0.3g Sodium: 397.7mg Total Carbohydrates: 25.6mg Fiber: 2.6g Protein: 2.0g

Blue Corn Cakes

1 1/4 cups blue cornmeal

2/3 cups unbleached flour

1/2 cup instant corn masa

1 1/2 teaspoons baking powder

1/2 teaspoon salt

1/4 cup canola oil

1/4 cup honey

1 1/4 cups soymilk

Mix dry ingredients together in a medium-sized mixing bowl. Make a well in the center and add wet ingredients. Stir only until mixed. Spoon mixture onto a hot griddle or skillet that has been oiled or sprayed with nonstick cooking spray. When bubbles form, flip over with a spatula and cook on the other side. Cook until lightly browned. Serve warm with pure maple syrup or your favorite topping.

These are hardy pancakes. If you would like them to be lighter and fluffier, then omit the instant corn masa and replace it with unbleached wheat flour or soy flour. You can also serve this as a savory dish for brunch or supper. Just top them with your favorite beans, salsa, and soy sour cream. —Cinda

Yield: 16 3-inch corn cakes

(Per corn cake) Calories: 125   Total Fat: 4.2g   Saturated Fat: 0.3g   Sodium: 177.3mg   Total Carbohydrates: 21.7mg   Fiber: 1.5g   Protein: 1.4g

Buckwheat & Flax Pancakes

Mix dry ingredients in a small bowl. Slowly add wet ingredients and stir until mixed well. Heat frying pan to medium heat. Oil or coat pan with nonstick cooking spray. Pour batter in 5-inch circles and cook until bubbles appear on the top of the pancake. Flip pancake with a spatula. Brown the other side and remove from pan. Serve hot with your favorite topping.

On Sunday mornings, my family loves to eat pancakes and waffles topped with warm homemade blueberry topping. This is a light and fluffy (not to mention healthy) pancake. You can use this recipe to make great waffles too! And if you happen to have any leftovers, they freeze well. —Cinda

3/4 cup whole wheat flour

1/2 cup buckwheat flour

2 teaspoons baking powder

2 tablespoons brown sugar

1 tablespoon flaxseed

1/2 teaspoon salt

1/4 teaspoon cinnamon

1 teaspoon pure vanilla extract

2 tablespoons canola oil

1 1/4 cups soymilk

Yield: 6 5-inch pancakes

(Per pancake) Calories: 173   Total Fat: 6.5g   Saturated Fat: 0.6g   Sodium: 572.4mg   Total Carbohydrates: 25.7mg   Fiber: 3.4g   Protein: 4.5g

Banana Nut Pancakes WITH PINEAPPLE SAUCE

1 medium-sized ripe
  banana

1 tablespoon canola oil

1 teaspoon pure vanilla
  extract

2 tablespoons pure maple
  syrup

1 cup whole wheat flour

1/4 teaspoon sea salt

1 1/2 teaspoons baking
  powder

1/8 teaspoon ground
  cinnamon

1/4 cup pecan pieces

Pineapple sauce
  (recipe below)

Toasted coconut for
  garnish

Strawberry for garnish

PINEAPPLE SAUCE

1 tablespoon cornstarch

1 tablespoon water

1/2 cup pineapple juice

2 tablespoons orange juice

Mash banana with a potato masher in a medium-sized bowl. Add canola oil, pure maple syrup, and pure vanilla extract. Mix dry ingredients together and slowly stir into wet ingredients. Gently stir until blended. Heat a large frying pan to medium heat and coat with nonstick cooking spray. For each pancake, pour 1/4 cup of batter into pan and spread to make a round pancake. Fry until golden on both sides. Serve pancakes with hot pineapple sauce on top. Garnish with toasted coconut and a sliced strawberry.

For pineapple sauce: In a small saucepan, mix cornstarch and water together until smooth. Add pineapple juice and orange juice and cook over medium heat, stirring constantly until it thickens.

My husband is a quiet man and doesn't comment much on his food. But when he tasted these pancakes he expressed more than once how delicious they were. I love to create recipes that bring a smile to his face. Enjoy! —Linda

Yield: 8 4-inch pancakes with sauce

(Per pancake) Calories: 121 Total Fat: 4.5g Saturated Fat: 0.3g Sodium: 141.8mg Total Carbohydrates: 18.8mg Fiber: 2.5g Protein: 2.7g
(Per serving sauce) Calories: 14 Total Fat: 0g Saturated Fat: 0g Sodium: 0.3mg Total Carbohydrates: 3.5mg Fiber: 0.1g Protein: 0.1g

Potato Latkes

Shred raw potatoes with a hand grater into a bowl. Transfer to a food processor and process slightly. You should still be able to see some shreds of potato. Return potatoes to mixing bowl and add remaining ingredients. Mix together. Add enough oil to a medium frying pan to cover the bottom of the pan and heat over medium heat. Test oil temperature by dropping a small piece of potato in the pan. When there is an immediate sizzle, the oil is hot and ready. Spoon approximately 1/4 cup potato mixture into frying pan. Fry until golden and crispy. Turn with a fork and fry second side until golden. Remove from pan and place on a platter covered with paper towels.

Our grandma Micheff always made the best potato pancakes, and she inspired this recipe. Grandma used eggs, but I was determined to find a way to make them without. These are surprisingly close to Grandma's, except that I added onion. I really like the extra flavor it gives! These are great for breakfast with scrambled tofu, but really and truly, I love them for any meal! For a healthier version, bake instead of frying. Spray a baking sheet with nonstick cooking spray. Place latke mixture 2 inches apart on sheet. Bake at 400 degrees for 10 to 15 minutes. Turn with a spatula and bake another 10 to 15 minutes until golden and crispy! —Brenda

2 medium raw potatoes, shredded

2 tablespoons all-purpose flour

1/2 teaspoon salt

1/2 teaspoon baking powder

1 tablespoon minced onion

Canola oil

Yield: 6 3-inch latkes

(Per latke) Calories: 51 Total Fat: 0g Saturated Fat: 0g Sodium: 228.9mg Total Carbohydrates: 11.8mg Fiber: 0.7g Protein: 1.0g

Potato Pancakes

1 cup raw, diced potatoes

1/2 cup water

1/2 teaspoon seasoned salt

1/4 teaspoon sea salt

1/2 teaspoon onion powder

1/4 cup raw, diced onion

1/2 cup whole wheat flour

Put all ingredients in the blender except for the whole wheat flour. Blend until smooth and pour into a medium-sized bowl. Mix in whole wheat flour. In a hot skillet coated with a small amount of olive oil, canola oil, or nonstick cooking spray, put 1/4 cup of batter and spread to make a 6-inch pancake. Fry until golden brown on both sides. Serve while the pancakes are hot.

These are some of my husband's favorite pancakes. I serve the pancakes with scrambled tofu and fresh fruit. Mmm, mmm, good! —Linda

Yield: 6 6-inch pancakes

(Per pancake) Calories: 69   Total Fat: 0.3g   Saturated Fat: 0g   Sodium: 142.4mg   Total Carbohydrates: 15.0mg   Fiber: 1.7g   Protein: 2.2g

Breakfast Potatoes

Wash and drain tofu and crumble into small pieces in a medium bowl. Add salts, onion powder, and sliced vegan hot dogs, and mix well. Set aside.

Heat olive oil in a medium-sized frying pan over medium heat. Add onions and sauté until they are almost clear. Add shredded potatoes. Add tofu mixture to the onions and potatoes and fry until potatoes are a golden brown.

The potatoes will cook down to about half the original amount. This breakfast can be prepared in 10 to 15 minutes. Serve it with toast and a colorful fruit salad. —Linda

1 cup water-packed tofu

1/4 teaspoon sea salt

1/4 teaspoon seasoned salt

1/4 teaspoon onion powder

1/2 cup sliced vegan hot dogs

1 tablespoon diced onions

1 tablespoon extra virgin olive oil

2 cups frozen shredded potatoes

Yield: 4 1/2-cup servings

(Per serving) Calories: 142   Total Fat: 4.6g   Saturated Fat: 0.7g   Sodium: 359.4mg   Total Carbohydrates: 20.0mg   Fiber: 1.5g   Protein: 6.7g

Grandma's Breakfast Hash

2 medium potatoes,
   cooked and cubed

1 teaspoon extra virgin
   olive oil

1/2 cup diced sweet onion

1/2 cup diced red bell
   pepper

1 cup chopped fresh
   spinach

Cayenne pepper to taste

Salt to taste

Boil or bake the potatoes until tender. Heat a medium-sized frying pan to medium and coat with nonstick cooking spray. Add extra virgin olive oil, onion, red bell pepper, and cubed potatoes. Sauté until onions are clear. Add spinach, cayenne pepper, and salt. Continue sautéing until potatoes are browned and slightly crispy. Serve hot.

This dish is quick, easy, and very tasty. You can add tofu, mushrooms, zucchini, or yellow summer squash. I think it turns out differently every time I make it! My husband, Joel, likes to make this with the kids for a quick dinner. With the three of them all adding their favorite ingredients, it gets pretty creative! —Cinda

Yield: 2 1-cup servings

(Per serving) Calories: 168   Total Fat: 2.6g   Saturated Fat: 0.4g   Sodium: 19.3mg   Total Carbohydrates: 34.3mg   Fiber: 4.1g   Protein: 3.7g

Picante Tofu Scramble

Heat a large nonstick skillet over medium heat. Coat with nonstick cooking spray. Add onion, red pepper, and carrot. Sauté until onions are clear. (You may need to re-spray the pan once or twice during sautéing to avoid sticking and burning.) When onions are clear, add fresh garlic, spices, and torn corn tortillas. Continue to sauté for 1 minute more. Add tofu and hot sauce and cook about 5 minutes or until tofu is slightly browned. Serve warm with your favorite salsa.

It is no secret that my family likes food with a lot of spice! You can omit the hot sauce or add just a dash, if you prefer your food a little more mild. I like to serve this in corn tortilla cups. Just gently (to avoid tearing) place corn tortillas into muffin tins. Spray with nonstick cooking spray and bake in a 375-degree oven for about 5 minutes or until crisp. Garnish each with salsa, Tofutti Sour Supreme, and black olives. —Cinda

1 medium onion, chopped

1 medium red bell pepper, diced

1 medium carrot, peeled and shredded

1 clove garlic, minced

1 teaspoon ground cumin

1/2 teaspoon ground turmeric

4 corn tortillas, torn in small- to medium-sized pieces

1 12.3-ounce package firm Mori-Nu Tofu or water-packed tofu, cubed or mashed

1/2 teaspoon hot sauce

Salt to taste

Salsa to taste

Yield: 4 3/4-cup servings

(Per serving) Calories: 145   Total Fat: 3.3g   Saturated Fat: 0.5g   Sodium: 63.1mg   Total Carbohydrates: 21.9mg   Fiber: 3.1g   Protein: 8.4g

Joel's Famous Hot Cereal

2 cups water

1/8 teaspoon salt

1/3 cup 8- or 10-grain hot cereal mix

1/2 cup quick oats

1/4 cup dried cranberries

1/4 cup dried cherries or blueberries

In a small saucepan, add water, salt, and multigrain hot cereal mix. Bring to a boil, then cover and reduce heat. Cook on low for 10 minutes. Add the quick oats and dried fruit. Continue to cook with the lid on for another 5 minutes. Turn off heat and let it sit for 5 minutes. Serve hot.

My husband, Joel, makes this for me every Sabbath morning! He will sometimes add different dried fruits but this combination is my favorite. You could also add some of your favorite nuts or slice a fresh banana on top of your serving. —Cinda

Yield: 4 1/2-cup servings

(Per serving) Calories: 211   Total Fat: 1.1g   Saturated Fat: 0.4g   Sodium: 72.5mg   Total Carbohydrates: 48.7mg   Fiber: 2.9g   Protein: 2.2g

Maple Almond Granola

Mix the oats, almonds, and coconut together in a large bowl. Mix the water, oil, pure vanilla extract, and syrup together in another container and then slowly pour over the dry ingredients. Form clumps by squeezing the granola together with your hands. Put granola on a baking pan with sides. Bake at 250 degrees until lightly brown and crisp. Cool and store in an airtight container.

I left the salt out of this recipe on purpose because it is good without it and it is healthier that way. If you want to use some salt, add 1/8 teaspoon or less to the dry ingredients. My husband Jim likes to add raisins, blueberries, strawberries, bananas, and soymilk to his granola—and he thinks that this meal is fit for a king! —Linda

2 cups quick oats

1/4 cup sliced almonds

1/4 cup sweetened coconut

3 tablespoons hot water

3 tablespoons canola oil

1 tablespoon pure vanilla extract

2 tablespoons pure maple syrup

Yield: 4 1/2-cup servings

(Per serving) Calories: 240   Total Fat: 7.9g   Saturated Fat: 2.5g   Sodium: 16.1mg   Total Carbohydrates: 38.2mg   Fiber: 5.0g   Protein: 6.4g

Oatmeal Raisin Muffins

1 cup oats

1 1/2 cups soymilk

1 teaspoon pure vanilla extract

1/3 cup canola oil

1/2 cup pure maple syrup

1/4 cup honey

1 3/4 cups whole wheat pastry flour

1 teaspoon baking powder

1 teaspoon baking soda

1 tablespoon cornstarch

1/2 teaspoon salt

1/2 teaspoon + 1 teaspoon cinnamon

1/4 teaspoon cloves

1/2 cup raisins

1/2 cup brown sugar

In a mixing bowl, mix together oats, soymilk, pure vanilla extract, oil, pure maple syrup, and honey. Set aside. In another mixing bowl, combine flour, baking powder, baking soda, cornstarch, salt, 1/2 teaspoon cinnamon, cloves, and raisins. Mix well and then add to liquid ingredients. Stir just until all dry ingredients are moistened. Batter will be lumpy. Spoon batter in muffin tins lined with cupcake liners or spray muffin tins with nonstick cooking spray. Divide batter evenly between 12 muffin tins. In a small bowl, mix together 1 teaspoon cinnamon and brown sugar for topping. Sprinkle cinnamon-sugar mixture over each muffin. Bake in a preheated oven at 400 degrees for 15 to 18 minutes. To test doneness, insert a toothpick in the center of muffin. Muffin is done if toothpick comes out clean. Don't overbake or muffins will be dry and tough!

These moist muffins are delicious all by themselves or served with a fresh fruit salad. Try substituting dried cranberries for the raisins and adding walnuts. Also yummy! I make these ahead of time and put them in the freezer. Then they are ready to pop in the microwave. It's like making them fresh! —Brenda

Yield: 12 muffins

(Per muffin) Calories: 273   Total Fat: 7.1g   Saturated Fat: 0.6g   Sodium: 258.2mg   Total Carbohydrates: 51.3mg   Fiber: 3.5g   Protein: 3.2g

Honey Corn Bread Muffins

Mix all dry ingredients together in a medium-sized mixing bowl. Make a well in the middle and add all wet ingredients. Stir until just mixed. Pour batter equally into paper-lined 3-inch muffin tins. Add water to unfilled muffin sections so that your pan won't warp and the muffins won't overbake. If using a dark-colored muffin tin, reduce the temperature 25 degrees because the dark metal attracts more heat. Bake at 375 degrees for 15 to 18 minutes.

1/2 cup yellow cornmeal

1/2 cup unbleached flour

1 teaspoon baking powder

1/2 teaspoon salt

1/2 cup soymilk

1 tablespoon canola oil

2 tablespoons honey

Sometimes I like to add a couple tablespoons of whole kernel corn or a tablespoon of chopped jalapeño peppers—or both! Be careful not to overbake; muffins should be moist and tender. —Cinda

Yield: 6 3-inch muffins

(Per muffin) Calories: 129   Total Fat: 2.9g   Saturated Fat: 0.2g   Sodium: 231.1mg   Total Carbohydrates: 25.2mg   Fiber: 1.0g   Protein: 1.2g

Cinnamon & Raisin Bread

1 cup warm water

1/4 cup pure maple syrup

1/4 cup canola oil

1/4 cup applesauce

1/4 cup cooked oatmeal

1 teaspoon salt

1/4 cup raisins

1/4 cup diced, pitted prunes

1 tablespoon active dry yeast

3/4 cup + 1/4 cup + 2 cups white whole wheat flour

1 tablespoon high-gluten flour or vital gluten

1 1/2 teaspoons soy margarine

1 teaspoon cinnamon

2 tablespoons Florida Crystals

In a large bowl, add water, maple syrup, oil, applesauce, oatmeal, raisins, and prunes. Mix together. Add approximately 3/4 cup flour and mix one minute. Stir the yeast into 1/4 cup flour and 1 tablespoon high-gluten flour and stir into the wet mixture. Slowly add the rest of the flour until it makes a soft dough that does not stick to your hands.

Knead the dough 10 to 15 minutes. Take the dough out of the bowl and place it on the counter. Cover with a clean dishtowel and let it rise until it has doubled.

Punch the dough down. Gently stretch it into a rectangle about 1/2-inch thick. Spread the soy margarine on the dough. Sprinkle with cinnamon and Florida Crystals.

Roll the dough up into a tight roll. Turn the ends under and place in a 1 1/2-pound bread pan that has been sprayed with nonstick cooking spray. Place bread in or on a warm place, such as your stove top, and cover with a towel until the loaf is double in size.

Bake at 350 degrees for approximately 30 minutes until golden brown. Place the bread on a cooling rack or towel and cover with a lint-free cloth.

I love the smell of home-baked bread drifting through our home. It is the smell of welcome to anyone who comes to my door. Sometimes when our mailman comes to the door to deliver a package that would not fit in our mailbox, I give him a loaf of freshly baked bread. I love to see his eyes light up with surprise—just my way of passing on God's blessings to others. Make an extra loaf and pass on the blessings! —Linda

Yield: 1 loaf, approximately 20 1/2-inch slices

(Per slice) Calories: 130 Total Fat: 3.9g Saturated Fat: 0.5g Sodium: 104.0mg Total Carbohydrates: 22.2mg Fiber: 0.8g Protein: 0.7g

Trail Mix

Place the nuts on a glass plate and microwave for 30 to 45 seconds until fragrant. Set aside to cool. Mix remaining ingredients together and then add cooled nuts. Store in an airtight container until ready to use.

This is a great recipe to pack for lunches or to take backpacking. You can add more of your favorite dried fruit or nuts. This mix is not only fast and easy to put together, but it is also nutritious and so delicious! —Linda

1/2 cup whole almonds

1/2 cup pecan halves

1/2 cup walnut halves

1/2 cup granola

1/2 cup raisins

1/2 cup dried apricots

1/2 cup dried cranberries

1/2 cup carob chips

Yield: 8 1/2-cup servings

(Per serving) Calories: 312 Total Fat: 19.0g Saturated Fat: 5.4g Sodium: 9.0mg Total Carbohydrates: 34.9mg Fiber: 5.1g Protein: 6.1g

Vibrant Life Energy Bars

1/4 cup peanuts

1/4 cup almond slivers

1/4 cup raisins

1/4 cup dried cranberries

1/4 cup dried apricots

1/4 cup sunflower seed
kernels

1 cup quick or old-
fashioned oats

1 1/4 cups rice cereal
(such as Rice Krispies)

1/2 cup smooth peanut
butter

1/4 cup honey

1/4 cup pure maple syrup

2 tablespoons vital wheat
gluten

1/2 teaspoon pure vanilla
extract

In a large bowl, combine peanuts, almonds, raisins, cranberries, apricots, sunflower seed kernels, oats, and rice cereal. Mix well and set aside. In a medium saucepan, combine peanut butter, honey, and maple syrup. Heat and stir until melted and smooth. Add vital wheat gluten. Stir until smooth. Do not bring to boil. Stir in pure vanilla extract and then pour over dry ingredients. Stir well and pour into an 8 x 8-inch pan that has been sprayed with nonstick cooking spray. Pat mixture down firmly into pan. Cut into 12 bar-shaped pieces. When the bars have cooled, wrap individually in plastic wrap.

These bars are ready to eat as soon as they have cooled, although I even like them warm! My sisters and I write the food articles for Vibrant Life, an awesome magazine promoting a healthy life style. I created this recipe for their annual 5-K "Fun Run" and we had so much fun handing these energy-packed bars out to all the runners! —Brenda

Yield: 12 bars

(Per bar) Calories: 170   Total Fat: 6.2g   Saturated Fat: 0.9g   Sodium: 46.5mg   Total Carbohydrates: 26.9mg   Fiber: 2.3g   Protein: 4.0g

Salads &
Sandwiches

Veggie Oat
Burgers
p. 51

Tomato Succotash
Salad
p. 41

Butternut
Pecan Salad
p. 36

Crispy
Oven Fries
p. 78

Roasted Vegetable
Sandwiches
p. 49

Almond
Broccoli Salad
p. 44

Butternut Pecan Salad

1 1/2 teaspoons lemon juice

1/2 cup orange juice

1/4 cup canola oil

2 teaspoons honey

1/2 teaspoon celery salt

1/2 teaspoon prepared mustard

4 cups washed, drained, bite-sized pieces of romaine lettuce

1/2 cup toasted pecans

1/2 cup dried cranberries

1 cup baked and cubed butternut squash

In a small mixing bowl, whisk together lemon juice, orange juice, oil, honey, celery salt, and mustard. Whisk until smooth. Set dressing aside in refrigerator.

Combine lettuce, pecans, cranberries, and squash in mixing bowl. Drizzle with dressing, toss well, and place on individual chilled plates or serve family style in a chilled glass salad bowl. Garnish with extra cranberries.

This salad has a mouthwatering, tangy citrus dressing that complements and intensifies the flavor of the squash! Try experimenting with different kinds of nuts and dried fruit. I've also used different types of lettuce, as well as baby spinach. I love this for a meal all by itself! —Brenda

Yield: 4 1-cup servings

(Per serving) Calories: 313 Total Fat: 23.1g Saturated Fat: 1.8g Sodium: 211.8mg Total Carbohydrates: 29.7mg Fiber: 3.2g Protein: 2.5g

Orange Almond Salad

In a large bowl, combine lettuce, spinach, almonds, pineapple, mandarin oranges, scallion, and avocado. Drizzle with 1/2 cup dressing. Save leftover dressing in a sealed container for more salads later!

For dressing: In a small mixing bowl, whisk together dressing ingredients. Stir until smooth. Set dressing aside in refrigerator.

This amazing, tangy dressing can be made the day before. I like my dressing cold, so this is a good option for me. If you do not want leftover dressing, cut recipe in half. For an extra-special touch, put your salad plates in the freezer and bring out just before serving. I like to serve this favorite salad to company or at special family dinners. Enjoy! —Brenda

2 cups washed, drained, bite-sized pieces of romaine lettuce

2 cups washed and drained baby spinach

1/2 cup toasted slivered almonds

1/2 cup pineapple tidbits

1/2 cup mandarin oranges

1 tablespoon minced scallion (include green stems)

1 medium avocado, peeled and cut into small cubes

1/2 cup lemon poppy seed dressing (recipe below)

LEMON POPPY SEED DRESSING

2/3 cup canola oil

1/2 cup sugar

1/3 cup lemon juice

2 teaspoons poppy seeds

1/2 teaspoon salt

1 teaspoon prepared mustard

Yield: 4 1 1/2-cup servings with dressing; dressing recipe is 1 1/2 cups

(Per serving) Calories: 321   Total Fat: 25.5g   Saturated Fat: 2.3g   Sodium: 101.1mg   Total Carbohydrates: 22.7mg   Fiber: 6.0g   Protein: 4.8g
(Per 2 tablespoons dressing) Calories: 68   Total Fat: 6.0g   Saturated Fat: 0.4g   Sodium: 39.9mg   Total Carbohydrates: 4.2mg   Fiber: 0g   Protein: 0g

Rainbow Vegetable Salad

1/4 cup lemon juice

1 tablespoon extra virgin olive oil

1 tablespoon sugar

1/8 teaspoon salt

1/2 cup black-eyed peas

1/2 cup slightly cooked and cooled frozen green peas

1/2 cup canned French-style green beans

1/2 cup drained canned pimentos (do not rinse)

1/2 cup fresh or canned corn

1/2 cup diced red bell peppers

2 cups washed, drained, bite-sized pieces of romaine lettuce

In a small mixing bowl, whisk together lemon juice, olive oil, sugar, and salt. Stir until sugar is dissolved. Set aside.

In a large bowl, combine black-eyed peas, green peas, green beans, pimentos, corn, and red bell peppers. Add dressing, toss together, and mix well. Refrigerate 1 to 2 hours or overnight. Serve over a bed of romaine lettuce.

My sister Linda is famous for saying "color your plate like a rainbow," so I created this recipe in her honor! It certainly covers all the bases with "color," which means lots of nutrients! You can substitute other vegetables, such as black beans, garbanzo beans, black olives, butter beans, etc. Just add your favorite vegetable and make it a new recipe! The only thing missing is some nice homemade wheat bread! Wow! What a meal! —Brenda

Yield: 6 1/2-cup servings

(Per serving) Calories: 82   Total Fat: 2.6g   Saturated Fat: 0.4g   Sodium: 55.6mg   Total Carbohydrates: 13.7mg   Fiber: 3.2g   Protein: 2.9g

Marathon Salad

Combine edamame, chickpeas, zucchini, and carrot in a medium-sized mixing bowl. In a smaller bowl, combine the fresh lemon juice, olive oil, and seasonings. Whisk until well blended. Pour over the beans and vegetables and stir well. Serve over a bed of torn romaine lettuce.

My husband, Joel, has run quite a few marathons, including the Marine Corps and Boston marathons. When he is training for them, he needs extra nutrition for energy that will go the distance. I decided to call this salad "Marathon Salad" because after you eat it, you should be able to run a marathon! Well, maybe not the whole 26 miles, but at least around the block.
—Cinda

1/2 cup shelled and cooked edamame (fresh soybeans)

1/2 cup canned chickpeas, drained and rinsed

1/2 cup chopped zucchini

1/2 cup shredded carrot

2 tablespoons fresh lemon juice

2 tablespoons extra virgin olive oil

1/8 teaspoon cayenne pepper

1/4 teaspoon salt

1 tablespoon chopped fresh basil (optional)

2 cups washed, drained, bite-sized pieces of romaine lettuce

Yield: 4 servings

(Per serving) Calories: 141 Total Fat: 8.7g Saturated Fat: 1.1g Sodium: 223.6mg Total Carbohydrates: 12.6mg Fiber: 3.4g Protein: 5.0g

Mexican Fiesta Salad

1 cup elbow macaroni pasta

1 cup black beans, drained and rinsed

1 cup chopped tomatoes (I use grape tomatoes)

1 cup chopped zucchini

1/2 cup sliced black olives

1 cup frozen or fresh corn

1/2 cup Tofutti Sour Supreme

1/2 cup mild or medium salsa

1 tablespoon chopped jalapeño peppers

1 tablespoon lime juice

Salt to taste

1 tablespoon chopped fresh parsley (may use dried)

Romaine lettuce to taste

Tortilla chips to taste

Cook pasta in salted boiling water according to package directions until al dente—tender, yet slightly chewy. Drain and rinse with cold water. Put pasta in a large mixing bowl and add black beans, tomatoes, zucchini, and black olives. Toss gently to mix. Spray a small sauté pan with nonstick cooking spray and add corn. Sauté on medium heat until corn is browned. (Make sure you put a lid on the pan as the corn literally pops out of the pan during the sautéing!) When browned, let cool a little and then add to the pasta mixture. In a small mixing bowl, stir together Tofutti Sour Supreme, salsa, jalapeños, lime juice, and salt to taste. Mix well and pour over pasta and vegetables. Toss gently until well mixed. Serve over a bed of shredded romaine lettuce and top with crushed tortilla chips.

This salad is a meal by itself! It is packed with lots of veggies plus black beans for protein. You could also add diced avocado right before serving. For a little more flavor, use vegetable seasoning instead of salt. This lasts for a couple of days in the refrigerator—if you have any leftovers to save! —Cinda

Yield: 7 1-cup servings

(Per serving) Calories: 162   Total Fat: 3.9g   Saturated Fat: 1.2g   Sodium: 200.5mg   Total Carbohydrates: 27.6mg   Fiber: 3.4g   Protein: 5.2g

Tomato Succotash Salad

Spray a small skillet with nonstick cooking spray. Add corn and sauté until lightly browned. Remove from heat and add cooked lima beans. In a small bowl, mix olive oil, lemon juice, oregano, pepper, and salt. Pour over corn and lima beans and stir until mixed. Set aside. Hollow out 4 medium tomatoes. Fill each hollow tomato with 1/2 cup of the succotash and serve. Refrigerate and serve cold if desired.

I live in the South, and succotash is quite popular here. But Mom used to make succotash for our family all the time—and we lived in the Midwest then! You don't have to put the salad into the tomato cups, but it does make it extra special. You could also use chopped chives instead of the fresh oregano for a little different flavor. —Cinda

1 cup frozen lima beans, cooked

2 cups fresh or frozen corn kernels

1 tablespoon extra virgin olive oil

1 tablespoon fresh lemon juice

1 teaspoon chopped fresh oregano

1/8 teaspoon cayenne pepper

Salt to taste

4 medium tomatoes

Yield: 4 1/2-cup servings

(Per serving) Calories: 167   Total Fat: 4.3g   Saturated Fat: 0.6g   Sodium: 20.2mg   Total Carbohydrates: 29.8mg   Fiber: 6.3g   Protein: 6.2g

Waldorf Coleslaw

1 cup shredded cabbage

1/2 cup shredded carrot

1/2 cup chopped walnuts

1/2 cup diced apple

1/2 cup chopped celery

2 tablespoons Grapeseed
Oil Vegenaise

1 tablespoon honey

1/2 teaspoon poppy seeds

1/2 teaspoon soymilk

Combine cabbage, carrot, walnuts, apple, and celery in a medium mixing bowl and set aside. In a small mixing bowl, whisk together Grapeseed Vegenaise, honey, poppy seeds, and soymilk until well blended. Pour over the cabbage mixture and stir until all ingredients are well coated with the dressing. Serve immediately or refrigerate until ready to serve.

This salad is wonderful for a brunch, light supper, or even a picnic. For individual servings, I hollow out a red apple and then fill it with the coleslaw. You can sprinkle a few chopped walnuts and grated carrot at the base of the apple. —Cinda

Yield: 2 3/4-cup servings

(Per serving) Calories: 252 Total Fat: 19.4g Saturated Fat: 2.3g Sodium: 90.3mg Total Carbohydrates: 18.8mg Fiber: 3.2g Protein: 3.8g

Strawberry Pecan Salad

Place pecans on a glass plate and microwave them on high for 4 to 5 minutes until toasted. They will firm as they cool. Set aside.

Combine field greens and lettuce. On 3 individual salad plates put 1/2 cup of lettuce. Decorate the top with strawberries, mandarin oranges, blueberries, canned pineapple, and pecans. Serve with strawberry dressing.

This salad is great for that extra-special occasion. Try substituting nuts such as walnuts, almonds, or cashews. It is also good with grated coconut on top! —*Linda*

For strawberry dressing: Partially thaw strawberries in the microwave on high for approximately 1 minute. Put in blender and add all the other ingredients. Blend until smooth.

This creamy dressing is also good served over fresh fruit with granola sprinkled on top. Mmm, mmm, good! —*Linda*

1/4 cup whole pecans, roasted

1/2 cup mixed field greens

1 cup romaine lettuce pieces

1/2 cup sliced fresh strawberries

1/4 cup mandarin orange sections

1/4 cup blueberries

1/4 cup canned pineapple tidbits (optional)

Strawberry dressing (recipe below)

STRAWBERRY DRESSING

1/4 cup frozen strawberries

1/4 cup Grapeseed Oil Vegenaise

1/4 cup cold water

1 tablespoon soymilk powder

1 1/2 tablespoons pure maple syrup

Yield: 3 1-cup servings salad; 10 2-tablespoon servings dressing

(Per serving salad) Calories: 82 Total Fat: 6.1g Saturated Fat: 0.5g Sodium: 3.3mg Total Carbohydrates: 7.2mg Fiber: 2.3g Protein: 1.4g
(Per serving dressing) Calories: 47 Total Fat: 3.8g Saturated Fat: 0.6g Sodium: 34.5mg Total Carbohydrates: 2.8mg Fiber: 0.1g Protein: 0g

Almond Broccoli Salad

1 cup broccoli florets

1 cup tomato pieces

1/2 cup whole black olives

2 tablespoons sliced
   almonds

Zesty dill dressing
   (recipe below)

ZESTY DILL DRESSING

1 tablespoon Grapeseed
   Oil Vegenaise

1 tablespoon Tofutti Sour
   Supreme

1 tablespoon cold water

1/4 teaspoon Lemony
   Dill Zest

1/4 teaspoon All-Purpose
   Veggie Salt

In a medium salad bowl, combine all salad ingredients except dressing. Toss. Serve salad with the dressing on the side so that people can control the amount they eat.

For dressing: Whisk all the ingredients together until well blended. Put the dressing in a small glass bowl and serve along with the salad.

This salad is not only colorful but delicious! I love the Lemony Dill Zest seasoning from The Vegetarian Express. It has a wonderful flavor! You will find where to purchase it on our resource page. —Linda

Yield: 5 1/2-cup servings salad; 3 1-tablespoon servings dressing

(Per serving salad) Calories: 39 Total Fat: 2.7g Saturated Fat: 0.3g Sodium: 122.7mg Total Carbohydrates: 3.4mg Fiber: 1.1g Protein: 1.3g
(Per serving dressing) Calories: 46 Total Fat: 4.0g Saturated Fat: 0.9g Sodium: 137.6mg Total Carbohydrates: 1.9mg Fiber: 0g Protein: 0.2g

Artichoke Salad

On two plates, spread the lettuce. Layer the other ingredients onto the lettuce. Garnish with shredded veggie chicken or gluten strips. Serve with your favorite dressing.

This salad makes a full meal for two. As a side dish, just follow the instructions above and divide onto small salad plates. Serve with your favorite pasta, garlic bread, and dessert. I keep washed romaine lettuce stored in a plastic container and extra veggies on hand. I also keep my table set at all times so that if guests stop by we are ready to invite them for a meal. When we plan so that we are always ready for the special guests that God sends us, we can relax and enjoy the blessings of friendship. —Linda

For dressing: Put all ingredients in the blender and blend until smooth. Chill before serving.

This dressing can be used on haystacks, tacos, salads, and any way that you would use a ranch dressing. It will keep approximately one week in a cold refrigerator. It's a good idea to check the temperature of your refrigerator from time to time. Unsafe bacterial growth and accelerated food spoilage occurs at 41 degrees and above. —Linda

2 cups washed, drained, bite-sized pieces of romaine lettuce

1 tomato, wedged

1/4 cup shredded carrots

1/4 cup kidney beans, drained and rinsed

1/4 cup garbanzos, drained and rinsed

1/4 cup water-packed artichokes

1/4 cup shredded red cabbage

1/4 cup shredded veggie chicken or gluten of your choice

2 black olives for garnish

Linda's light ranch dressing (recipe below) or dressing of your choice

LINDA'S LIGHT RANCH DRESSING

1/2 12.3-ounce package Mori-Nu Tofu

2 tablespoons cold water

2 tablespoons Vegenaise

2 tablespoons Tofutti Sour Supreme

1/2 teaspoon fresh squeezed lemon juice

1/2 teaspoon onion powder

1 teaspoon Saucy Ranch Seasoning

1/2 teaspoon All-Purpose Veggie Salt

Yield: 5 1-cup servings salad; 9 2-tablespoon servings dressing

(Per serving salad) Calories: 43   Total Fat: 0.5g   Saturated Fat: 0.1g   Sodium: 29.0mg   Total Carbohydrates: 7.7mg   Fiber: 2.6g   Protein: 2.9g
(Per serving dressing) Calories: 43   Total Fat: 3.2g   Saturated Fat: 0.7g   Sodium: 90.3mg   Total Carbohydrates: 1.8mg   Fiber: 0g   Protein: 1.5g

Tijuana Salad

1 teaspoon canola oil

1/4 teaspoon All-Purpose Veggie Salt

1/4 cup shredded gluten (I prefer a light-colored gluten for this dish.)

1 cup washed, drained, bite-sized pieces of romaine lettuce

1/2 cup cooked brown rice (optional)

1 cup undrained chili beans

1/2 cup fresh, frozen, or canned sweet corn

1/2 cup tomato pieces

1/2 cup sliced black olives

1 tablespoon minced fresh chives

Tofutti Sour Supreme

Salsa

In a medium-sized skillet, add the teaspoon of canola oil and gluten and seasoning. Fry until golden brown and set aside. Spread the lettuce onto a glass serving plate. Spread on the rice (if using) and then chili beans, leaving some of the lettuce showing all the way around. Sprinkle corn and then tomatoes on top. Place shredded gluten in the middle of the salad. Sprinkle olives and chives on top. Garnish with a dollop of Tofutti Sour Supreme and serve with mild salsa.

The All-Purpose Veggie Salt that I use comes from the Vegetarian Express and can be found on our resource page. This is a perfect salad for two. Just add dinner rolls and homemade cookies. —Linda

Yield: 3 generous 1-cup servings

(Per serving) Calories: 127 Total Fat: 3.7g Saturated Fat: 0.3g Sodium: 571.0mg Total Carbohydrates: 21.4mg Fiber: 5.5g Protein: 6.6g

Mock Egg Salad Sandwiches

Rinse tofu well. Wrap in paper towels and place on a plate. Place heavy object on top and let sit for 10 minutes until firm and free of liquid. Set aside. In a mixing bowl, combine Vegenaise, La Chikky Seasoning, turmeric, salt, and pickle relish. Mix well then add drained tofu. Mix gently making sure not to overmix. There should be pea-sized clumps of tofu. Set aside.

Spread Vegenaise on bread. Spread mock egg salad mixture on four slices of the bread. Add lettuce and tomato. Top with another bread slice. Slice diagonally. Serve with sweet pickles and oven fries.

My husband loves egg salad sandwiches, and the first time I served this recipe to him, he didn't even know the difference! Mock egg salad makes a wonderful appetizer too. Just spread on minirye sandwich squares or pumpernickel crackers and garnish with sliced green or black olives. You can also serve as a dip with a variety of crackers or small bread slices. You can use other brands of chicken-style seasoning but my favorite is La Chikky by The Vegetarian Express. —Brenda

1 16-ounce package extra-firm, water-packed tofu

1/2 cup Grapeseed Oil Vegenaise + more to spread on bread

2 1/2 teaspoons La Chikky Seasoning

1/4 teaspoon turmeric

Salt to taste

1/2 cup sweet pickle relish

8 slices whole wheat bread

Lettuce leaves

Tomato, sliced

Yield: filling for 4 sandwiches

(Per sandwich) Calories: 318 Total Fat: 24.4g Saturated Fat: 4.0g Sodium: 579.1mg Total Carbohydrates: 15.1mg Fiber: 0.7g Protein: 9.1g

"Ricotta" Tomato Sandwiches

1 16-ounce package
    extra-firm,
    water-packed tofu

3 tablespoons Grapeseed
    Oil Vegenaise

2 tablespoons lemon juice

3/4 teaspoon salt

4 slices French bread or
    bread of your choice

1 tablespoon extra virgin
    olive oil

4 pieces fresh basil leaves
    (optional)

4 slices fresh tomato

Rinse tofu well. Wrap in paper towels and place on a plate. Place heavy object on top and let sit for 10 minutes until firm and free of liquid. Set aside. In a mixing bowl, combine Vegenaise, lemon juice, and salt. Add tofu. With a large serving fork or potato masher, crumble it gently into pea-sized clumps. Do not overmix. Set aside.

Brush one side of bread slices with olive oil. Place oiled side down on hot skillet. Place a lid on top to steam bread slightly. Remove lid and continue toasting oiled side of bread until golden and slightly crispy. Remove from skillet and place on platter. Spread "ricotta" mixture over toasted bread. Top with sliced fresh tomato and basil leaves, if desired.

My friends Mark and Conna Bond shared this "ricotta" recipe with me. I came up with this sandwich idea for a perfect way to use it. Mark and Conna eat the "ricotta" and vegetarian bacon bits on baked potatoes. They also use it to fill lasagna. I have to admit they have me hooked too. I love it on this sandwich and all by itself is pretty good too! —Brenda

Yield: 4 open-faced sandwiches

(Per sandwich) Calories: 367   Total Fat: 17.8g   Saturated Fat: 2.8g   Sodium: 814.3mg   Total Carbohydrates: 37.6mg   Fiber: 2.5g   Protein: 14.8g

Roasted Vegetable Sandwiches

Preheat oven to 400 degrees. On a large baking sheet, spread all vegetables. Sprinkle with pinch Italian seasoning and salt. Drizzle with olive oil. Roast 30 to 40 minutes. Turn every 15 minutes so that vegetables brown evenly. Vegetables are roasted when they can be penetrated with a fork and edges are slightly darkened. Set aside.

Slice buns in half and brush inside pieces with olive oil. Toast oiled side of buns on a hot skillet until golden and crispy. Spread prepared mustard on toasted sides. Layer on vegetables, dividing them evenly between the sandwiches. Place second half of bun on top of each sandwich, slice down the middle, and serve with oven fries.

This sandwich's flavor can almost fool your palate into thinking the vegetables were roasted on a grill! I sometimes try different kinds of breads, but the French rolls are my favorite. Don't be tempted to skip toasting the buns, as this really adds to the overall dining experience! —Brenda

4 strips eggplant peeled and sliced to 4-inch slices and 1/4-inch thick

1/2 cup of 1/4-inch thick sliced zucchini

1/2 cup very thinly sliced red bell pepper

1/2 cup slivered red onion

1 tablespoon extra virgin olive oil

Italian seasoning to taste

Salt to taste

2 whole wheat French buns or hoagie rolls

Prepared mustard

Yield: 2 sandwiches

(Per serving filling) Calories: 108   Total Fat: 7.2g   Saturated Fat: 1.0g   Sodium: 6.6mg   Total Carbohydrates: 11.3mg   Fiber: 5.7g   Protein: 2.1g

Gringo Meal in a Pocket

2/3 cup cooked brown rice

1 cup canned black beans, drained and rinsed

1 cup frozen or fresh corn kernels

1 4-ounce can diced green chiles

1/4 teaspoon salt or to taste

1/3 cup salsa + more for topping

1/2 cup chopped fresh tomatoes

2 pita bread rounds, halved

4 romaine lettuce leaves

Tofutti Sour Supreme

Combine rice, beans, corn, chiles, salt, salsa, and tomatoes in a medium-sized skillet. Stir over medium heat until hot. Line pita bread halves with a lettuce leaf. Fill pita with brown rice mixture and top with Tofutti Sour Supreme and salsa.

This is a great recipe for picnics or your lunchbox because the filling is also delicious when eaten cold. Keep the filling and toppings separate and assemble right before serving. I like to serve this buffet-style so everyone can make his or her own pocket meal. You can have lots of toppings on your buffet, such as fresh avocado or guacamole, sliced olives, and chopped fresh chives. —Cinda

Yield: 4 1/2-pita sandwiches

(Per serving filling) Calories: 151   Total Fat: 0.9g   Saturated Fat: 0.2g   Sodium: 290.9mg   Total Carbohydrates: 31.4mg   Fiber: 6.1g   Protein: 6.3g

Veggie Oat Burgers

In a medium skillet, heat olive oil and then add onion, carrot, celery, and zucchini. Sauté over medium heat until onion is clear. Remove from heat and add brown rice, oats, cornstarch, garlic powder, cumin, cayenne, Brewer's yeast, and Vege-Sal. Mix well. With a fork, mash tofu into fine pieces and mix into rice-oat mixture. In a small bowl, stir together water and Liquid Aminos. Pour over rice-oat mixture and stir until evenly moistened. Shape into eight patties approximately four inches in diameter. Dredge each patty into the bread crumbs, coating both sides. Place patties on a baking sheet that has been sprayed with nonstick cooking spray. Also spray the tops of each patty. Bake in a 375-degree oven for 15 minutes. Turn the patties over, spray the tops with cooking spray and bake another 20 minutes. Remove from oven and let them sit for 5 minutes. They freeze quite well.

These patties are not only good in a sandwich, but they are great for an entrée too. I like to serve them with mashed potatoes and gravy. They are also nice to take on a picnic or in your lunch because they taste good hot or cold. —Cinda

1 tablespoon extra virgin olive oil

1/2 cup minced onion

1/4 cup grated carrot

1/4 cup minced celery

1/4 cup grated zucchini

1 cup cooked brown rice

1 1/2 cups quick oats

1/2 teaspoon garlic powder

1/2 teaspoon cumin powder

1/8 teaspoon cayenne pepper

1 tablespoon Brewer's yeast flakes

2 tablespoons cornstarch

1 teaspoon Vege-Sal or your favorite all-purpose vegetable seasoning

1 12.3-ounce package of Mori-Nu tofu, firm or extra-firm

1/2 cup water

2 tablespoons Bragg Liquid Aminos

Bread crumbs to dredge patties

Yield: 8 patties

(Per patty) Calories: 145   Total Fat: 3.4g   Saturated Fat: 0.5g   Sodium: 561.9mg   Total Carbohydrates: 21.4mg   Fiber: 3.1g   Protein: 7.8g

Open-faced BLT

2 sliced and toasted bagels

1/4 cup Tofutti Better
Than Cream Cheese

1 tablespoon Grapeseed
Oil Vegenaise

1 teaspoon veggie bacon
bits

1/2 teaspoon All-Purpose
Veggie Salt

4 tablespoons shredded
green leaf lettuce

8 slices Roma tomatoes

Mix cream cheese, Grapeseed Oil Vegenaise, bacon bits, and All-Purpose Veggie Salt together. Spread on each half of toasted bagels. Put sliced tomatoes on each half and sprinkle with shredded lettuce. Serve with Crispy Oven Fries (p. 78) and your favorite dessert.

This sandwich is yummy and is great to pack in lunches. Just add some fresh fruit and your favorite cookie—now that's a lunch! —Linda

Yield: 4 open-faced sandwiches

(Per sandwich) Calories: 153 Total Fat: 5.5g Saturated Fat: 1.5g Sodium: 358.2mg Total Carbohydrates: 21.5mg Fiber: 1.2g Protein: 4.0g

Soups & Stews

Poor Man's
Stew
p. 73

Split Pea Soup
p. 62

Butternut
Squash Soup
p. 56

Garden
Gazpacho
p. 61

Curried Black
Bean Soup
p. 63

Butternut Squash Soup

1 tablespoon soy
  margarine

1 medium onion, minced

1/4 cup minced celery

1/4 cup minced Granny
  Smith apple

1 cup baked, mashed
  butternut squash

1 1/2 cup vegetable broth

Pinch nutmeg

1/2 teaspoon cinnamon +
  extra for garnish

1/4 teaspoon salt

1 cup soymilk

1/2 cup Silk brand creamer
  (soymilk creamer)

Cinnamon to taste

In a medium saucepan, combine margarine, onion, celery, and apple. Sauté until onion is clear. Add baked squash and mix well. Let cool slightly. Pulse in food processor until very smooth. Return to saucepan. Stir in broth, nutmeg, cinnamon, salt, and soymilk. Let simmer for several hours on the stove at low heat or pour into a Crock-Pot and cook on low for 2 to 4 hours. When ready to serve, stir in the Silk creamer and top with a dash of cinnamon.

I love butternut squash just about any way you can fix it, so I'm always experimenting with new recipes. You don't have to wait until autumn to enjoy this soup since butternut squash is available year-round at grocery stores. Sometimes I substitute coconut milk for the soymilk. —Brenda

Yield: 4 1-cup servings

(Per serving) Calories: 114   Total Fat: 5.3g   Saturated Fat: 1.2g   Sodium: 541.8mg   Total Carbohydrates: 15.4mg   Fiber: 0.9g   Protein: 1.7g

Pasta Fagioli

In a large pot, heat olive oil and sauté onion, celery, garlic, oregano, and salt until onion is clear. Add remaining ingredients except for the pasta and bring to a boil. Turn down to low heat and let simmer for 1 to 2 hours until flavors are well blended and vegetables are tender. Increase heat and return to a boil, then add pasta. Cook until pasta is tender. Remove from heat and serve.

I like to serve this with crusty Italian bread and a Greek salad. For extra zip, add 1/4 teaspoon of cayenne pepper. You can use any of your favorite beans: pinto, kidney, garbanzo, butter beans, etc. Try adding other pastas, but use a mini size so the pasta doesn't overwhelm the soup! —Brenda

1 tablespoon extra virgin olive oil

1 medium onion, diced

1/2 cup minced celery

2 cloves garlic, minced

1 teaspoon salt

1/2 teaspoon oregano

4 cups water

2 cups canned diced tomatoes

1 cup tomato puree

1/2 cup canned great northern beans, drained and rinsed

1/2 cup canned black beans, drained and rinsed

2 cups frozen mixed vegetables

1 bay leaf

1 teaspoon sugar

1 teaspoon soy sauce

1 tablespoon minced fresh parsley

3 vegetarian chicken bouillon cubes

1/2 cup ditalini (mini pasta tubes)

Yield: 8 1-cup servings

(Per serving) Calories: 195   Total Fat: 2.7g   Saturated Fat: 0.4g   Sodium: 708.0mg   Total Carbohydrates: 37.9mg   Fiber: 8.6g   Protein: 8.5g

Taco Soup

1 medium onion, minced

2 cloves garlic, minced

1 tablespoon extra virgin olive oil

1 12-ounce package Yves Ground Round Veggie Original or vegetarian burger of your choice

2 cups canned diced tomatoes

1 to 2 cups water

1 cup canned pinto beans, drained and rinsed

1 cup canned black beans, drained and rinsed

1 14-ounce can creamed corn

1/2 cup diced green chiles

1 1.2-ounce package taco seasoning mix

2 tablespoons Saucy Ranch Seasoning

1/4 cup picante sauce

Heat olive oil in a medium saucepan. Add onion and garlic and sauté until onion is clear. Add remaining ingredients and bring to a boil. Simmer for approximately one hour. Serve hot!

Taco soup is spicy without being too hot. If you want to kick it up a notch, add 2 to 3 tablespoons hot sauce or toss in a few diced jalapeño peppers or crushed red pepper flakes. It's also good with a sprinkle of Saucy Ranch Seasoning from The Vegetarian Express. Occasionally, I serve taco soup over rice! —Brenda

Yield: 6 1-cup servings

(Per serving) Calories: 252   Total Fat: 3.6g   Saturated Fat: 0.5g   Sodium: 825.5mg   Total Carbohydrates: 40.8mg   Fiber: 9.6g   Protein: 17.9g

Tomato Bisque

In large pot, melt soy margarine. Sauté onion, carrots, and celery in the margarine until tender. Remove from heat and cool slightly. Put into blender or food processor and add 1/4 cup water. Blend until smooth. Return blended mixture to pot and add remaining ingredients. Simmer, stirring occasionally, until bullion cubes have dissolved and soup is hot.

For a delicious lunch, serve this hot soup with your favorite sandwich. Tomato bisque has a nice, smooth, blended flavor and is so fast and easy to make! You can substitute dried basil, but it will have a different taste. Still good, just different! —Brenda

2 tablespoons soy margarine

1 medium onion, minced

2 medium carrots, peeled and minced

1/2 cup minced celery

1/4 cup water

2 cups vegetable broth

1 1/2 cups tomato puree

2 teaspoons minced fresh sweet basil

1 cup water

1 cup soymilk

1 tablespoon honey

2 vegetarian chicken bouillon cubes

1/2 teaspoon salt or to taste

Yield: 4 1-cup servings

Calories: 104   Total Fat: 4.2g   Saturated Fat: 1.4g   Sodium: 854.5mg   Total Carbohydrates: 16.3mg   Fiber: 2.2g   Protein: 2.0g

Creamy Carrot Soup

2 cups water

2 tablespoons McKay's
  Chicken Seasoning
  (Vegan Special)

1 tablespoon Island Spice
  Jamaica All Seasoning

2 cups diced carrots

1 cup diced potato

1/2 cup chopped onion

1/2 teaspoon minced fresh
  ginger

3/4 cup soymilk

Soy sour cream to taste

Chives or parsley

In a medium saucepan, combine water, seasonings, carrots, potato, onion, and ginger. Bring to a boil. Reduce heat and simmer for 20 to 25 minutes until vegetables are tender. Remove from heat. Put 2 cups of the soup in a blender or food processor and blend until smooth. Return to pan and mix well with remaining vegetables. Add soymilk and stir until combined. Serve hot with a dollop of soy sour cream and a sprinkle of chives or parsley.

When our daughter Catie was little, she loved carrots. We would have to hide the carrots until she had eaten the other food served at the meal, or she would fill up on them! So this soup always reminds me of her. She could definitely fill up on this soup—and you can too! —Cinda

Yield: 4 1-cup servings

(Per serving) Calories: 75   Total Fat: 0.6g   Saturated Fat: 0g   Sodium: 890.6mg   Total Carbohydrates: 16.2mg   Fiber: 2.5g   Protein: 1.7g

Garden Gazpacho

Add all ingredients together into a medium bowl and stir until combined. Chill for 1 to 2 hours or overnight before serving. Serve cold.

My husband, Joel, loves to garden. We all enjoy the fresh tomatoes and vegetables he grows. He taught our son David how to plant a garden too! From the time David was 8 years old, he kept fresh herbs growing right out our back door for me to use whenever I needed them. This gazpacho was inspired from all those fresh herbs and vegetables they harvested. It is great for lunch or dinner on those hot summer days. You can serve it with a dollop of soy sour cream and a sprinkle of fresh herbs. You may substitute red tomato if you do not have yellow. —Cinda

1/2 cup cooked corn

1 yellow tomato, seeded and chopped

1 cup chopped raw zucchini

1/2 cup diced carrots, cooked until crunchy tender

1/2 cup cooked peas

1/2 cup diced, unpeeled English or pickling cucumber

2 cups V8 Vegetable Juice

2 teaspoons lime juice

2 tablespoons fresh basil or parsley

1/4 teaspoon salt or to taste

1/8 teaspoon cayenne pepper

Yield: 4 1-cup servings

(Per serving) Calories: 80 Total Fat: 0.6g Saturated Fat: 0.1g Sodium: 243.4mg Total Carbohydrates: 17.5mg Fiber: 3.5g Protein: 3.2g

Split Pea Soup

1 tablespoon extra virgin olive oil

1 small onion, chopped

2 teaspoons minced garlic fresh

1 1/2 cups split peas

1/2 cup barley

1 cup diced carrots

1 cup diced celery

2 bay leaves

2 teaspoons crushed basil leaves

2 teaspoons marjoram

1 teaspoon salt or to taste

1 teaspoon Vege-Sal

7 cups water

Heat olive oil in a large saucepan. Sauté onion in oil until onion is clear. Add remaining ingredients and bring to a boil. Reduce heat to low and simmer for 1 hour or until split peas are tender. You will need to stir several times during cooking. You can add more water if the soup gets too thick.

When cooked, blend 4 cups of the soup in a blender or food processor until smooth. Return to saucepan and stir until mixed with the rest of the soup. Serve hot.

This soup gets thicker the longer it sits, especially when you refrigerate the leftovers. Just add more water and seasonings if needed when reheating.
—Cinda

Yield: 8 1-cup servings

(Per serving) Calories: 195 Total Fat: 2.5g Saturated Fat: 0.4g Sodium: 358.5mg Total Carbohydrates: 33.8mg Fiber: 12.3g Protein: 10.9g

Curried Black Bean Soup

Heat oil in a medium saucepan. Sauté garlic and onion until onions are clear. Add some of the water if mixture becomes too dry. Put remaining ingredients in the pan and cook 15 to 20 minutes. Serve hot.

My husband loves soup and sandwiches. Sometimes to spice up this soup I add 1/4 cup mild salsa. That makes it even better! This dish can also be served over brown rice. Just add 3/4 cup more of the canned black beans, serve over rice, and you have a complete meal! —Linda

1/2 teaspoon extra virgin olive oil

1/2 teaspoon minced fresh garlic

1/2 cup diced onions

1 cup water

1 cup canned diced petite tomatoes

1 cup canned black beans, drained and rinsed

1/2 teaspoon sea salt

1/2 teaspoon onion powder

1/4 teaspoon curry powder

Yield: 3 1-cup servings

(Per serving) Calories: 107 Total Fat: 1.2g Saturated Fat: 0.2g Sodium: 318.1mg Total Carbohydrates: 19.2mg Fiber: 6.2g Protein: 5.9g

Fiesta Rice Soup

3 cups water

1/2 cup diced onions

1/2 cup diced carrots

1/2 cup diced celery

1/2 cup mild salsa

1/2 cup canned dark red kidney beans, drained and rinsed

1/2 cup chopped frozen or fresh spinach

1 tablespoon McKay's Chicken Seasoning (Vegan Special)

1 teaspoon All-Purpose Veggie Salt

1/2 teaspoon onion powder

1/2 cup instant brown rice

Stir all ingredients except rice into a medium-sized pot. Cook on medium-high heat until the vegetables are almost tender, approximately 15 minutes. Add instant brown rice. Cook for about 8 to 10 minutes more. Serve hot!

My family loves soup—even for breakfast. Brown rice and beans not only taste good but are a healthful way to start the day! This soup is good garnished with a tablespoon of Tofutti Sour Supreme and a sprig of cilantro or fresh parsley. Sometimes I make a pan of corn bread to go with our soup. That always puts a smile on my mother-in-law's face. I love putting smiles on the faces in my family! —Linda

Yield: 4 1-cup servings

(Per serving) Calories: 149   Total Fat: 0.7g   Saturated Fat: 0g   Sodium: 720.5mg   Total Carbohydrates: 30.9mg   Fiber: 2.5g   Protein: 4.5g

Garden Fresh Veggie Soup

Put water, tomatoes, seasonings, and salt in a 2-quart pan on the stove and set the temperature to medium high. Add vegetables to broth in the pan. Cook about 30 minutes until vegetables are well done.

My husband and I love eating simple suppers. We take our meal outside and enjoy watching the birds and deer that come and visit our backyard. I love all the wonderful things in nature that God gave us to help rest our minds. You will be blessed too as you spend some time with your family eating good food and enjoying each other's company. —Linda

2 cups hot water

1 cup canned diced tomatoes with juice

1 teaspoon McKay's Beef Seasoning (Vegan Special)

1 teaspoon All-Purpose Veggie Salt

1/4 teaspoon sea salt

1/4 teaspoon onion powder

1/8 teaspoon garlic powder or one crushed clove fresh garlic

1/4 cup diced onion

1/4 cup diced celery

1/2 cup diced carrots

1 cup diced cabbage

1/2 cup diced green beans

3/4 cup diced summer squash

1/2 cup diced broccoli

Yield: 3 1-cup servings

(Per serving) Calories: 57 Total Fat: 0.2g Saturated Fat: 0g Sodium: 626.7mg Total Carbohydrates: 12.8mg Fiber: 3.8g Protein: 2.5g

Red Lentil Soup

2 3/4 cups water

1/2 cup uncooked red lentils

1/2 teaspoon Saucy Ranch Seasoning

1/2 teaspoon McKay's Chicken Seasoning (Vegan Special)

1/2 teaspoon dried or fresh parsley

1/4 cup diced red pepper

1/4 cup sliced green onions

1/2 teaspoon sea salt, optional

Tofutti Sour Supreme

Chives

In a medium pan, add all ingredients except the Tofutti Sour Supreme. Bring to a boil. Lower the heat and simmer until lentils are mushy, stirring occasionally. The soup will have a creamy appearance. Garnish with Tofutti Sour Supreme and a sprinkle of chives. Serve hot!

Sometimes we serve our lentil soup on top of steaming brown rice. Add a colorful salad, some home-baked bread, and you will have a nutritious and delicious meal for your family. My husband loves leftovers so I try to make extra so we can have it for more than one meal. Just double the recipe and share the blessings! Enjoy! —Linda

Yield: 2 1-cup servings

(Per serving) Calories: 174 Total Fat: 0.5g Saturated Fat: 0.1g Sodium: 157.0mg Total Carbohydrates: 30.0mg Fiber: 15.4g Protein: 13.9g

Rotini Tomato Soup

Put all the ingredients in a medium saucepan. Bring to a boil and reduce to simmer. Cook 10 to 15 minutes until onions and spinach are done, stirring occasionally. Serve hot.

I shared this recipe with my friends Dave and Shirley Rhode. They gave it their thumbs-up. I used my mom's home-canned tomatoes in this recipe and that made it extra special for us, as we love what Mom makes! My brother Ken and Mom grow lots of tomatoes in their garden and share them with all their neighbors. Blessings to you and your family as you benefit from God's wonderful gifts of food. —Linda

2 cups canned diced tomatoes

2 tablespoons sliced green onions

1/4 cup fresh or frozen diced spinach

1/2 cup canned kidney beans, drained and rinsed

1/2 cup cooked rotini pasta

1/4 teaspoon sea salt

1/2 teaspoon Saucy Ranch Seasoning

Yield: 2 1-cup servings

(Per serving) Calories: 187 Total Fat: 0.6g Saturated Fat: 0.1g Sodium: 352.8mg Total Carbohydrates: 38.4mg Fiber: 7.6g Protein: 8.7g

Smokey Mountain Chili

1 tablespoon extra virgin olive oil

1 medium onion, minced

2 cloves garlic, minced

2 cups canned tomatoes diced

1 cup water

1 teaspoon McKay's Beef Seasoning (Vegan Special)

2 tablespoons chili powder

1 tablespoon brown sugar

1 tablespoon vegan Worcestershire sauce

1 teaspoon ground cumin

1/2 teaspoon salt

2 cups canned chili beans (do not drain)

1 teaspoon crushed red pepper flakes or to taste

Heat olive oil in medium-sized saucepan over medium heat. Sauté onion in olive oil until clear. Add garlic and sauté for 1 minute. Add remaining ingredients. Bring to a boil. Reduce heat to very low and simmer for 1 to 2 hours.

If you want to decrease the sodium content in any of our recipes calling for canned tomatoes, be sure to look for "low sodium" on the label. If you don't like things too hot, then omit the red pepper flakes. If you like it really spicy, then add more! I love chili year-round and usually pair it with corn bread. For a whole new dish, pour this entire recipe into a 9 x 13-inch glass baking dish and then take any corn bread recipe and pour over the top! Bake 25 to 30 minutes until corn bread is golden and starting to crack on top. Now you have two recipes in one! —Brenda

Yield: 6 1-cup servings

(Per serving) Calories: 133   Total Fat: 3.4g   Saturated Fat: 0.4g   Sodium: 670.9mg   Total Carbohydrates: 20.7mg   Fiber: 7.5g   Protein: 5.6g

Sweet Potato Stew

Heat olive oil in a medium saucepan. Sauté onion and garlic until onion is clear. Add all remaining ingredients and bring to a boil. Reduce heat to very low and simmer for 1 to 2 hours until sweet potatoes are tender and the flavor of the stew is well blended.

This nice, thick stew can be made several days before serving. It keeps well in the refrigerator for 3 to 4 days. I love serving it with warm biscuits and a green salad. On busy days I put this stew in the Crock-Pot and let it cook slowly all day! My husband loves to come home and smell the delicious aroma, and I love having supper ready! —Brenda

1 medium onion, minced

2 cloves garlic, minced

2 tablespoons extra virgin olive oil

2 cups vegetable broth

1 1/2 teaspoons lemon juice

1 medium sweet potato, peeled and diced into small pieces (approximately 2 cups)

3/4 cup red or yellow lentils, rinsed and drained

1/2 cup minced peeled carrots

1 1/2 cups canned diced tomatoes

1/4 cup smooth peanut butter

2 tablespoons honey

1 tablespoon curry powder

1 teaspoon salt

1/8 teaspoon cayenne pepper

1/8 teaspoon ground ginger

1/4 teaspoon ground cumin

Yield: 6 1-cup servings

(Per serving) Calories: 328 Total Fat: 15.6g Saturated Fat: 3.0g Sodium: 660.2mg Total Carbohydrates: 37.7mg Fiber: 11.3g Protein: 13.5g

Mi Casa Stew

1 15-ounce can black
beans, drained but
not rinsed

1 15-ounce can pinto
beans, drained but
not rinsed

1 14 1/2-ounce can
Mexican-style stewed
tomatoes

2 cups vegetable broth

1 cup frozen or fresh corn

2 cups diced potatoes

1 cup frozen or fresh cut
green beans

1 teaspoon cumin

Salt to taste

1 cup mild salsa

Soy sour cream

In a medium pan, combine all ingredients and stir. Bring to a boil. Cover, reduce heat, and simmer for 30 minutes, stirring occasionally. Garnish with soy sour cream if desired.

This quick stew's spiciness can be controlled by the hotness of the salsa. If you do not have vegetable broth, season 2 cups of water with an all-purpose vegetable seasoning. This stew is good served over brown rice or polenta. My husband, Joel, and our kids, David and Catie, gave this stew their thumbs-up. I think your family will too! —Cinda

Yield: 8 1-cup servings

(Per serving) Calories: 211 Total Fat: 0.9g Saturated Fat: 0.2g Sodium: 476.9mg Total Carbohydrates: 41.7mg Fiber: 11.5g Protein: 11.2g

Taj Mahal Stew

In a medium-sized stockpot, heat olive oil. Sauté onion and ginger in oil until onion is clear. Add garlic, cumin, turmeric, coriander, cayenne, and curry powder. Sauté 1 minute more. Add the remaining ingredients and bring to a boil. Cover, reduce heat, and simmer for 30 to 40 minutes, stirring occasionally, until lentils are soft. Serve hot.

My family loves Indian food! This thick stew is filled with the exotic flavors and aromas typical of that country. You can eat Taj Mahal Stew as is or spoon it over bowls of steaming brown rice. If you like things a bit spicier, then use a hotter curry powder or increase the cayenne pepper. —Cinda

1 tablespoon extra virgin olive oil

1 small onion, chopped

1 teaspoon minced fresh ginger

1 teaspoon minced fresh garlic

1/2 teaspoon ground cumin

1/2 teaspoon ground turmeric

1/2 teaspoon ground coriander

1/8 teaspoon cayenne pepper

1 teaspoon curry powder

1/2 cup dried lentils, rinsed and drained

2 cups chopped fresh spinach

2 cups water

1 tablespoon McKay's Chicken Seasoning (Vegan Special)

1 14 1/2-ounce can stewed tomatoes

1/2 teaspoon salt or to taste

Yield: 4 3/4-cup servings

(Per serving) Calories: 162 Total Fat: 3.9g Saturated Fat: 0.5g Sodium: 704.5mg Total Carbohydrates: 25.5mg Fiber: 9.9g Protein: 8.3g

Vegetable Stew

1 cup chopped onion

1 tablespoon extra virgin
   olive oil

2 cups slivered gluten

2 cups diced potatoes

1 cup sliced carrots

1 cup diced celery

1 cup frozen peas

2 cups hot water

1 tablespoon Vegex

1 teaspoon Vege-Sal

1 6-ounce can tomato
   paste

1 cup V8 Vegetable Juice

3/4 cup gluten or vegetable
   broth

1/2 cup ketchup

Salt to taste

Heat olive oil over medium heat in a medium-sized saucepan. Sauté onion until clear. Add gluten pieces and sauté another couple of minutes. Add potatoes, carrots, celery, and peas and stir together. In a 1-quart measuring cup, add the hot water. Dissolve Vegex in the water. Stir in Vege-Sal, tomato paste, V8 juice, broth, and ketchup. Pour into saucepan over vegetables and stir. Bring to a boil. Cover, reduce heat, and simmer for 40 to 45 minutes until vegetables are tender. Salt to taste and serve hot.

I love the rich tomato taste of this stew. I like to use my homemade gluten, but I also use Worthington Choplets when I am in a hurry and don't have any homemade gluten on hand. —Cinda

Yield: 7 1-cup servings

(Per serving) Calories: 135 Total Fat: 2.8g Saturated Fat: 0.4g Sodium: 697.0mg Total Carbohydrates: 22.9mg Fiber: 4.2g Protein: 6.8g

Poor Man's Stew

Put vegetables, gluten, Bragg Liquid Aminos, seasonings, and 2 cups cold water into a medium-sized pan and bring to a boil. Reduce heat, cover, and simmer for 20 to 25 minutes until vegetables are tender. In a small bowl, mix cornstarch and 1 tablespoon cold water together until smooth. Slowly stir into stew. Stir until stew thickens. Serve hot with your favorite dinner rolls and salad.

I like to serve this stew over homemade biscuits. My husband loves it just like it is. He even enjoys eating this stew for breakfast. We live at a youth camp where he does a lot of hard physical work so we start our day with prayer and a good hearty breakfast. It is amazing how God uses such simple ways to bless our lives. God is so good! —Linda

1/4 cup diced onions

1/4 cup sliced carrots

2 cups chopped fresh green beans

1 cup diced potatoes

1/4 cup chopped gluten

2 tablespoons Bragg Liquid Aminos

1/2 teaspoon onion powder

1/4 teaspoon sea salt

2 cups + 1 tablespoon cold water

1 tablespoon cornstarch

Yield: 2 1-cup servings

(Per serving) Calories: 104   Total Fat: 0.5g   Saturated Fat: 0.1g   Sodium: 1187.9mg   Total Carbohydrates: 22.4mg   Fiber: 5.4g   Protein: 4.6g

Entrées & Side Dishes

Spicy Arrabbiata
Sauce
p. 84

Stuffed
Peppers
p. 90

Enchiladas
Muy Buenas
p. 92

Italian Countryside
Secondo
p. 89

Pesto Mashed
Potatoes
p. 79

Crispy Oven Fries

2 cups raw French fry cut potatoes

1 tablespoon extra virgin olive oil

1 tablespoon Brewer's yeast flakes

1 teaspoon La Chikky Seasoning

1/2 teaspoon All-Purpose Veggie Salt

Put all ingredients in a mixing bowl and stir together. Spray a nonstick baking pan with nonstick cooking spray. Spread the seasoned fries on the tray. Bake at 400 degrees for 20 to 25 minutes until crispy. Serve hot!

I love French fries! Because they are so high in fat and not so good for my heart or body, I rarely eat them. My friends Radek and Helena Mekulasek shared their healthy version of French fries with me and I decided to make them using my favorite seasonings. Not only did I love them, but my family thought they were delicious too. Now when I make homemade veggie burgers for my family they get fries too! —Linda

Yield: 4 1/2-cup servings

(Per serving) Calories: 131 Total Fat: 3.5g Saturated Fat: 0.5g Sodium: 176.4mg Total Carbohydrates: 19.3mg Fiber: 3.5g Protein: 5.9g

Pesto Mashed Potatoes

In a medium saucepan, cook potatoes in salted boiling water until tender but firm. Drain and place in a mixing bowl. Add spinach, pesto, soymilk, and salt to taste. Blend with a mixer until smooth. Serve hot.

My daughter, Catie, and I love fresh basil. We are constantly looking for new ways to use it in our recipes. I always have a pot or two of basil growing inside and outside so that we can have it fresh year-round. We worked together creating this recipe using the fresh basil pesto. If you like a subtler pesto flavor, then just add a little less, making it according to your own taste. —Cinda

4 cups diced potatoes

1 cup chopped spinach

1/4 cup soymilk

4 to 5 tablespoons Florentine pesto (recipe on p. 104)

Salt to taste

Yield: 3 1-cup servings

(Per serving) Calories: 204 Total Fat: 13.2g Saturated Fat: 1.5g Sodium: 103.7mg Total Carbohydrates: 19.8mg Fiber: 3.0g Protein: 3.6g

Mashed Potato Casserole
WITH TOMATO CREAM SAUCE

4 cups diced raw potatoes

1 teaspoon salt + salt to taste

1 cup fresh whole wheat bread crumbs

1 cup walnuts

1 medium onion, minced

2 cloves garlic, minced

2 tablespoons + 1 tablespoon soy margarine

2 teaspoons cilantro leaves

2/3 cup vegetable stock

1 tablespoon cornstarch

1 cup cubed portobello mushrooms

1/4 cup canned roasted red bell peppers, chopped

Tomato cream sauce (recipe below)

TOMATO CREAM SAUCE

3 tablespoons tomato paste

1 teaspoon honey

2 teaspoons cilantro (dried leaves)

1 cup Silk brand creamer

1/4 teaspoon onion powder

Salt to taste

Preheat oven to 350 degrees. Place potatoes and salt in a large saucepan, cover with water, and bring to a boil. Reduce heat to medium and cook approximately 10 minutes until potatoes are tender. Drain water from potatoes and mash with a hand potato masher. Set aside.

In a food processor, place fresh slices of whole wheat bread and process into small crumbs to make one cup. Next process walnuts into small crumbs. Set aside.

Heat two tablespoons margarine in a large skillet. Sauté onion and garlic in margarine until translucent. Add cilantro, bread crumbs, and walnuts, and stir until well blended. Mix vegetable stock and cornstarch together and stir into bread crumb mixture. Cook for 1 to 2 minutes and then stir together with mashed potatoes and set aside. In a skillet, sauté mushrooms in remaining 1 tablespoon margarine until tender. Sprinkle with salt to taste. Set aside.

In a 1-quart casserole dish, place half of potato mixture and pat down. Spread mushrooms over potato mixture and top with roasted bell pepper. Top with remaining potato mixture and smooth with a rubber spatula. Cover with aluminum foil. Bake for 1 hour. Serve hot with tomato cream sauce on the side to drizzle over each individual serving.

This is one dish that is sure to please any potato lover and is filling enough to be the main meal! Just add a green vegetable and garden salad. You might want to double the recipe and invite your friends! —Brenda

For sauce: Mix together all ingredients and heat in a small saucepan. Simmer on low heat for five minutes. Serve hot!

This delicious sauce really enhances the flavor of this mashed potato casserole! You might even say it is "the icing on the cake"! Tastes like it cooked all day, and it really takes five minutes tops! —Brenda

Yield: 4 1-cup servings casserole; 4 1/4-cup servings sauce

(Per serving casserole) Calories: 199   Total Fat: 14.0g   Saturated Fat: 2.4g   Sodium: 405.0mg   Total Carbohydrates: 16.3mg   Fiber: 2.8g   Protein: 4.5g

(Per serving sauce) Calories: 39   Total Fat: 2.0g   Saturated Fat: 0g   Sodium: 25.8mg   Total Carbohydrates: 4.3mg   Fiber: 0.3g   Protein: 0.3g

Creamy Potato Bake

Microwave the frozen shredded potatoes for approximately 1 to 2 minutes until soft. Put onions, red pepper, mushrooms, and olive oil in a glass bowl with a lid and microwave for approximately 1 minute. Mix the cooked onions, red pepper, and mushrooms with the potatoes. Mix all the rest of the ingredients together and stir into potato mixture. Bake in a glass dish with a lid at 350 degrees for 30 to 35 minutes until hot and bubbly. Do not remove lid while potatoes are baking because the potatoes will dry out. Sprinkle with fresh chives and serve hot.

My mother-in-law loves potatoes—maybe not as much as my sister Cinda—but she sure does enjoy them. She gave these potatoes her thumbs-up. She is a really good cook, so I know when she likes something it must be good! Enjoy!
—Linda

2 cups frozen shredded potatoes

2 tablespoons minced green onions

2 tablespoons minced sweet red pepper

2 tablespoons minced fresh mushrooms

1 teaspoon extra virgin olive oil

1/4 cup Tofutti Sour Supreme

1/4 cup plain soymilk

1/4 teaspoon sea salt

1/4 teaspoon All-Purpose Veggie Salt

1/4 cup water

Fresh chives

Yield: 4 1/2-cup servings

(Per serving) Calories: 170 Total Fat: 4.8g Saturated Fat: 1.4g Sodium: 277.0mg Total Carbohydrates: 29.5mg Fiber: 3.5g Protein: 4.7g

Scalloped Mushroom Potatoes

1 medium onion, chopped

1 to 2 tablespoons canola oil

2 1/2 cups sliced mushrooms

4 medium potatoes, raw, peeled, and thinly sliced

1 to 2 teaspoon salt

2 1/2 cups soymilk

1/3 cup Wondra flour or very fine all-purpose flour

In a large saucepan, heat oil and sauté onion until clear. Add sliced mushrooms and continue sautéing until mushrooms change color. Remove from heat and set aside. In a 9 x 9-inch glass baking dish, place a layer of raw potatoes, then sprinkle with salt and add a layer of mushrooms and onions. Continue this until all ingredients have been layered in dish. Set aside.

In a container that has a tight-fitting lid, place soymilk and flour. (I use a glass canning jar.) Secure the lid, then shake vigorously until liquid is smooth. Pour over layered potatoes and mushrooms. Cover loosely with foil and bake at 375 degrees for approximately 45 minutes. Remove foil and continue baking for another 15 minutes. Top should be golden and slightly crusty. Serve hot!

My family loves potatoes, and I have fun trying new ways to fix them. Sometimes I add vegetables, such as fresh asparagus, corn, peas, or green beans to this dish. It turns into a new recipe. If you want to make your own "Wondra flour," it is easy to do. Just take all-purpose flour and put it in your blender. Blend for about 30 seconds and that's all it takes! Be prepared, though, for that fine flour dust that infiltrates the air when you take the lid off the blender. To avoid that, just let it sit for a few minutes "until the dust settles"! —Brenda

Yield: 6 1-cup servings

(Per serving) Calories: 191   Total Fat: 3.4g   Saturated Fat: 0.2g   Sodium: 367.3mg   Total Carbohydrates: 36.4mg   Fiber: 4.0g   Protein: 5.9g

Corn Bread Pudding

Preheat oven to 350 degrees. In a large mixing bowl, combine flour, cornmeal, sugar, salt, baking powder, and cornstarch. Make a well in the center and add remaining ingredients. Mix well by hand and pour into a 1-quart or 1.6-liter baking dish. Bake 45 to 50 minutes. Top should be golden with small cracks forming on top.

This is an old-fashioned Southern recipe, but its rich, moist, delicious corn flavor is sure to be a crowd-pleaser wherever you live! You can have all kinds of fun with this recipe by adding jalapeño peppers, pimentos, green chiles, black olives, and, oh, so many other ingredients! —Brenda

1/2 cup unbleached white or whole wheat flour

1/2 cup cornmeal

1/4 cup sugar

1/2 teaspoon salt

1 1/2 teaspoons baking powder

1 tablespoon cornstarch

1/2 cup soymilk

1 tablespoon canola oil

1/2 cup canned or fresh corn

1 15-ounce can creamed corn

1/2 cup Toffutti Sour Supreme

Yield: 4 1/2-cup servings

(Per serving) Calories: 190   Total Fat: 5.00g   Saturated Fat: 1.17g   Sodium: 279.11mg   Total Carbohydrates: 36.02mg   Fiber: 1.68g   Protein: 2.58g

Spicy Arrabbiata Sauce

1 medium onion, diced

1 to 2 tablespoons extra
virgin olive oil

3 cloves garlic, minced

1/2 cup minced celery

1/2 cup minced red bell
pepper

1/2 cup diced mushrooms

2 cups canned diced
tomatoes

1/2 cup water

1/2 cup vegetable broth

1/2 teaspoon ground basil

1/2 teaspoon ground
oregano

1/4 teaspoon red pepper
flakes (optional)

1/2 teaspoon Vegetarian
Express Roasted
Garlic & Red Bell
Pepper Zip

1 1/2 tablespoons sugar

1/2 teaspoon salt

2 tablespoons tomato paste

2 cups cooked pasta of
your choice

In a large saucepan, heat olive oil. Sauté onion until clear. Add celery, red bell pepper, mushrooms, and garlic and cook until vegetables are tender. Add all remaining ingredients except pasta. Bring to a boil and then lower heat to simmer. Simmer for 3 to 4 hours to really blend the flavors! Serve with cooked pasta of your choice!

My favorite pasta to serve this with is angel hair, but my husband would probably pick ziti. Some of my other favorites include bow tie, penne, and linguine. If you really like things spicy, add more of the red pepper flakes, and if you don't like spicy at all, then just omit them. I love to put this in a Crock-Pot and let it simmer all day long on the low setting. My son-in-law David tells me this is the real Italian way! —Brenda

Yield: 4 1/2-cup servings

(Per serving with pasta) Calories: 149   Total Fat: 2.2g   Saturated Fat: 0.3g   Sodium: 218.6mg   Total Carbohydrates: 28.5mg   Fiber: 2.5g   Protein: 4.5g

Melanzana Rotini

Cook pasta in salted boiling water according to package directions until al dente, tender but slightly chewy. Drain and reserve 1/4 cup of the water. Set both aside.

In a medium saucepan, heat olive oil and margarine over moderate heat. Add eggplant and garlic and sauté until eggplant is tender. Add chopped spinach, lemon juice, and salt to taste. Stir well and sauté for 2 minutes. Add pasta, pasta water, and spaghetti sauce. Stir until combined and serve hot.

Italy is one of my favorite places to visit. The restaurants are filled with pasta dishes that have only a few simple ingredients in them. Each region prepares them just a little different but always with the freshest vegetables and herbs.
—*Cinda*

1 cup whole wheat rotini pasta

1/2 cup to 3/4 cup spaghetti sauce

1/4 cup pasta water

1 tablespoon margarine

1 tablespoon extra virgin olive oil

1 teaspoon chopped garlic

2 cups peeled and cubed eggplant

1 cup chopped fresh spinach

1 tablespoon fresh lemon juice

Salt to taste

Yield: 2 1 1/2-cup servings

(Per serving) Calories: 377   Total Fat: 14.5g   Saturated Fat: 3.4g   Sodium: 249.0mg   Total Carbohydrates: 49.8mg   Fiber: 10.2g   Protein: 12.4g

Broccoli Pepper Stir-fry

1 tablespoon canola oil

1 clove garlic, crushed

1/2 cup teriyaki sauce (recipe below)

1/4 cup broccoli florets

1/4 cup julienne cut carrots

1/4 cup julienne cut onions

1/4 cup julienne cut sweet red pepper

1/4 cup Morningstar Farms Meal Starters Steak Strips or gluten of your choice

1/4 cup sliced mushrooms

1/2 teaspoon All-Purpose Veggie Salt

1/4 teaspoon sea salt

1 cup cooked brown rice

Cashews

TERIYAKI SAUCE

1/4 cup Bragg Liquid Aminos

1 tablespoon fresh grated ginger

3 tablespoons brown sugar

1 clove garlic, minced

1 cup + 1/4 cup cold water

2 tablespoons cornstarch

Stir-fry hints: Be sure to cut up all the vegetables to approximately the same size prior to cooking. A good stir-fry is made very quickly, and you won't have time to prepare the vegetables once you start. To keep stir-fry vegetables crisp and oil absorption low, the key is to have a very hot wok and use oil with a high smoke point. Many stir-fry dishes are made with peanut oil, but canola usually is not a problem. You can tell when the oil is hot by adding a drop of water. When the oil is hot enough, the water will pop into steam on contact. Also, be sure to use the freshest vegetables, and remember that certain vegetables cook faster than others—it all depends on their density and moisture content (the amount of water they hold). Start with vegetables such as carrots, green beans, and broccoli since they have a higher density of water. After these vegetables have been sautéed for a couple minutes, add the thinner, lower-density vegetables, such as snap peas, red peppers, mushrooms, and spinach.

In a medium-sized skillet over high heat, heat the oil. Add broccoli, carrots, onion, and garlic, stirring constantly for approximately 3 minutes. Add 1/2 cup teriyaki sauce, pepper, gluten strips, mushrooms, and salts. Continue stirring over high heat until vegetables are slightly crunchy. Serve over brown rice and sprinkle with cashews.

For teriyaki sauce: Combine Bragg Liquid Aminos, ginger, sugar, garlic, and 1 cup water in a medium sauce pan and bring to a boil. Stir constantly. Mix cornstarch and 1/4 cup water til smooth and add to sauce. Stir constantly until thickened.

We love the crunchy goodness of nuts with this stir-fry. If you are pressed for time, use your favorite teriyaki sauce. Serve with Brenda's Orange Almond Salad (p. 37) and Cinda's Peanut Butter Bars (p. 120). Enjoy! —Linda

Yield: 3 1/2-cup servings; teriyaki sauce recipe yields 1 cup

(Per serving with rice) Calories: 172   Total Fat: 5.5g   Saturated Fat: 0.5g   Sodium: 918.0mg   Total Carbohydrates: 27.9mg   Fiber: 1.9g   Protein: 3.4g

(Per teriyaki sauce recipe) Calories: 226   Total Fat: 0.1g   Saturated Fat: 0g   Sodium: 3618.8mg   Total Carbohydrates: 56.8mg   Fiber: 0.3g   Protein: 0.3g

Roasted Vegetable Couscous

Put all prepared vegetables in a bowl and toss with olive oil. Spray a baking sheet with nonstick cooking spray. Spread vegetables evenly on the pan. Sprinkle with salt. Roast in a 425-degree oven for 15 to 20 minutes until vegetables are tender and browned. Watch closely so they do not burn. Add garbanzo beans during the last 5 minutes.

Prepare couscous while vegetables are roasting. In a medium saucepan, bring water, La Chikky Seasoning, and salt to a boil. Stir in couscous. Cover and remove from heat. Let stand for 5 minutes or until all liquid is absorbed. Fluff couscous with a fork and place on a medium-sized serving platter. Top with roasted vegetables.

This is a very easy and versatile recipe. You can also add your favorite vegetables and some gluten pieces. The flavor of the roasted vegetables is so good that you don't need to add any other seasonings. —Cinda

1 cup 1 1/2-inch pieces fresh asparagus

1 cup thinly sliced carrot rounds

2 cups diced peeled eggplant

1 cup diced zucchini

1/2 cup slivered red bell pepper

1 cup sliced grape tomatoes

1 tablespoon extra virgin olive oil

1 cup canned garbanzo beans, rinsed and drained

1 tablespoon La Chikky Seasoning

1 1/2 cups water

1 cup couscous

Yield: 3 1-cup servings

(Per serving) Calories: 411   Total Fat: 6.8g   Saturated Fat: 0.9g   Sodium: 296.6mg   Total Carbohydrates: 73.4mg   Fiber: 12.5g   Protein: 15.3g

Vegetable Putu-Pap

4 cups + 1 1/2 cups water

1 14-ounce can creamed corn

1 teaspoon salt

2 teaspoons soy margarine

1 1/2 cups white cornmeal

1 tablespoon McKay's Chicken Seasoning (Vegan Special) or vegetable seasoning of your choice

Salt to taste

1 small onion, diced

1 cup sliced zucchini

1 cup sliced yellow squash

1 cup 1/2-inch pieces green beans

1 cup sliced peeled carrots

1 small sweet potato, peeled and cubed

1 cup spaghetti sauce

In a large pot, add 4 cups water, creamed corn, salt, and soy margarine. Bring to a boil and add cornmeal, stirring constantly. Stir 3 to 5 minutes over medium heat until thickened. Put half of the cornmeal mixture into an 8 x 8-inch baking dish that has been sprayed with nonstick cooking spray. Cover the remaining cornmeal mixture to keep it warm.

In a large saucepan, mix 1 1/2 cups water with the seasoning, and bring to a boil. Add onion and cook until clear. Add zucchini, squash, green beans, carrots, and sweet potato, and cook until tender yet firm. Drain vegetables and set aside. (I save the liquid and freeze it to use later in soups.)

Spread 1/2 cup of spaghetti sauce over cornmeal mixture in the baking dish. Then evenly distribute all the vegetables on top of the sauce. Evenly spread the remaining 1/2 cup of spaghetti sauce over the vegetables. Cover with the remaining cornmeal mixture, making sure to completely cover the vegetables. Bake at 375 degrees for 30 minutes until bubbly and hot. Cut into 6 squares and serve.

I went to South Africa with my sisters and loved the putu-pap I had while we were there. Everywhere we ate it, it seemed to be served just a little differently. When I made this for my husband, Joel, he loved it! The only thing he wanted me to add was a little more spice! You can sprinkle some of your favorite spices onto the vegetables before you add the remaining spaghetti sauce, if you like yours spicy. You can also serve it with extra spaghetti sauce to spoon over each individual serving. Joel thinks it makes great leftovers! —Cinda

Yield: 6 1-cup servings

(Per serving) Calories: 192   Total Fat: 2.7g   Saturated Fat: 0.7g   Sodium: 729.2mg   Total Carbohydrates: 40.7mg   Fiber: 4.6g   Protein: 4.6g

Italian Countryside Secondo

In a medium skillet, heat olive oil. Add carrots, zucchini, summer squash, onion, garlic, eggplant, and salt, and sauté until onion is clear and vegetables are tender. Remove from heat and add the fresh oregano, basil, diced tomatoes, and spaghetti sauce. Serve over bowls of hot polenta or your favorite pasta.

In Italian, secondo *means the "entrée," the main or second dish, and this dish certainly makes a healthy and delicious highlight to any meal. I like it equally as well over polenta or pasta. Serve it with a thick, hot slice of Italian bread, and it may make you feel like you are sitting in the Tuscan countryside watching the sun go down! Mama Mia! —Cinda*

1 tablespoon extra virgin olive oil

1 cup diced carrots

1 cup diced zucchini

1 cup diced yellow summer squash

2 cups 1- to 2-inch cubed and peeled eggplant

1/2 cup chopped onion

1 teaspoon minced fresh garlic

Salt to taste

1 cup diced fresh tomatoes

1/4 cup chopped fresh basil

1 tablespoon chopped fresh oregano

1 cup prepared spaghetti sauce

Polenta or pasta

Yield: 6 3/4-cup servings

(Per serving) Calories: 75   Total Fat: 2.9g   Saturated Fat: 0.4g   Sodium: 138.2mg   Total Carbohydrates: 11.5mg   Fiber: 3.5g   Protein: 2.1g

Stuffed Peppers

2 red, yellow, or orange peppers

1/2 cup diced onion

2 tablespoons olive oil

1/2 cup Yves Ground Round Veggie Original or vegetarian burger of your choice

1 teaspoon salt

1 cup uncooked brown rice

1 quart low sodium canned tomatoes

Remove and discard the tops, seeds, and membranes of the bell peppers. Heat olive oil in a medium-sized frying pan over medium heat. Add onions and sauté until they are translucent. Add the vegetarian burger and salt. Stir, add dry rice, and stir again. Spoon mixture into peppers and place in a small cooking pot. Pour canned tomatoes over the top, cover, and bring to a boil. Reduce heat and simmer for 1–2 hours until rice is tender, not mushy.

Serve these hot with green vegetables and fresh salad! I love to add crusty Italian bread served with olive oil for dipping! —Brenda

Yield: two stuffed peppers

(Per stuffed pepper) Calories: 548   Total Fat: 3.5g   Saturated Fat: 0.6g   Sodium: 1350.8mg   Total Carbohydrates: 114.0mg   Fiber: 16.6g   Protein: 20.6g

Mama's Meatloaf

In a large nonstick skillet, saute onion in margarine until clear. Add carrots, celery, pepper, and garlic. Sauté until vegetables are tender. Add rest of ingredients except for ketchup. Stir until mixture holds together well. Spray a 5 x 9-inch bread pan with nonstick cooking spray. Pat meatloaf down firmly. Spread ketchup on top. Bake at 375 degrees for 1 hour.

My husband was out of town when I created this recipe so I asked my Kids' Time *assistant, Brenda Abbott, and her coworker, Rhonda, to come over and do the taste test! On a scale of 1 to 10, they gave it a 20! The best part was that Rhonda wasn't prepared to "like vege food" but this dish changed her mind! —Brenda*

1 medium onion, minced

1/2 cup minced celery

2 cloves garlic, minced

2 tablespoons nonhydrogenated margarine

1/2 cup diced mushrooms

1/4 cup diced red bell pepper

1 cup shredded carrots

1 cup quick oats

1/2 cup finely chopped walnuts

1/4 cup sunflower seed kernels

1/2 teaspoon salt

1/4 teaspoon dried basil

1/4 teaspoon dried oregano

1/4 teaspoon Vegetarian Express Pepper-Like Seasoning

1 1/2 cups soft whole wheat bread crumbs

1/2 cup ketchup

Yield: 6 1 1/2-inch slices

(Per slice) Calories: 265.3 Total Fat: 14.4g Saturated Fat: 2.4g Sodium: 322.3mg Total Carbohydrates: 31.0mg Fiber: 5.0g Protein: 7.2g

Enchiladas Muy Buenas

1/2 cup broccoli, cut into small pieces

1/2 cup sliced mushrooms

1/2 cup chopped zucchini

1/2 cup chopped carrots

3 cups diced potatoes

1 tablespoon extra virgin olive oil

1/2 cup soymilk

Salt to taste

1 10-ounce can mild enchilada sauce

4 6-inch corn tortillas

In a medium mixing bowl, combine broccoli, mushrooms, zucchini, and carrots. Drizzle with olive oil and stir to coat all the vegetables. Spray a large baking sheet with nonstick cooking spray and spread vegetables evenly on the baking sheet. Sprinkle with salt and bake in a 400-degree oven for 15 to 20 minutes until vegetables are tender and lightly browned. Remove from oven and set aside.

Meanwhile, cook potatoes in salted water until tender. Drain and then mash, stirring in the 1/2 cup of soymilk. Stir in the roasted vegetables.

In a dry, nonstick skillet over moderate heat, quickly heat each tortilla on both sides to make them soft. Immediately dip tortilla in enchilada sauce, making sure to coat both sides. Put about 1/2 cup of vegetable filling into each tortilla. Roll up. Place seam-side down in a small baking dish. Pour extra sauce over the top and bake in a 375-degree oven for 20 minutes.

I love potatoes and am always looking for ways to use them in my recipes. This one my whole family liked! You can add diced jalapeños if you want to spice the enchiladas up a bit. These freeze well, so you could make up a double batch and have some frozen for those spur of the moment meals! —Cinda

Yield: 4 enchiladas

(Per enchilada) Calories: 169   Total Fat: 5.0g   Saturated Fat: 0.6g   Sodium: 401.0mg   Total Carbohydrates: 28.2mg   Fiber: 4.5g   Protein: 3.9g

Papa's Mushroom Patties

Put brown rice, veggie burger, and quick oats into a mixing bowl and mix until blended. Set aside. In a glass bowl, put mushrooms and olive oil and cover. Microwave approximately 1 minute until mushrooms are done. Add to burger mixture. In a blender, put onions, Liquid Aminos, McKay's Beef Seasoning, and water. Blend until smooth and then add to burger mixture. Stir until well blended.

Spray a baking pan with nonstick cooking spray. On the pan, form five burgers using 1/4 cup of burger mixture for each. Lightly pat. Spray the top of each burger with nonstick cooking spray and bake in a preheated oven at 350 degrees for 25 to 30 minutes until golden brown. Halfway through baking turn the patties over. Serve plain or with your favorite gravy.

When I created these patties, my husband, Jim, loved them so much I named them "Papa's Patties," because he is affectionately called Papa by our two grandkids, Jack and Janie. I serve the patties with scalloped potatoes, a fresh green salad, and homemade wheat bread. Brown rice is so good for us that I like to cook up extra rice and keep in it in my refrigerator. There are so many recipes you can make using brown rice. These patties also make great veggie burgers! I like to make extra to store in my freezer for a quick lunch. —Linda

- 1/2 cup cooked brown rice
- 1/2 cup Worthington Vegetarian Burger or burger of your choice
- 2 tablespoons quick oats
- 1/4 cup diced fresh mushrooms
- 1 teaspoon extra virgin olive oil
- 1/4 cup diced onions
- 1 teaspoon Bragg Liquid Aminos or soy sauce
- 1/2 teaspoon McKay's Beef Seasoning (Vegan Special)
- 3 tablespoons water

Yield: 5 patties

(Per patty) Calories: 60   Total Fat: 1.4g   Saturated Fat: 0.2g   Sodium: 188.4mg   Total Carbohydrates: 8.4mg   Fiber: 1.3g   Protein: 3.9g

Potato Spinach Patties

2 tablespoons minced onion

1 teaspoon extra virgin olive oil

1 cup frozen shredded potatoes

1/2 cup frozen, chopped, cooked, and drained spinach

1/4 cup cooked oatmeal

1 tablespoon Grapeseed Oil Vegenaise

1 tablespoon Tofutti Better Than Cream Cheese

1/4 teaspoon McKay's Chicken Seasoning (Vegan Special)

1/8 teaspoon sea salt

1/4 cup finely crushed, seasoned bread crumbs

Put onions and olive oil in a glass dish with a lid and microwave for approximately 1 minute until onions are clear. Thaw potatoes in the microwave in a medium-sized mixing bowl. Add onions, spinach, oatmeal, Vegenaise, cream cheese, McKay's Chicken Seasoning, and salt to potatoes. Mix together until well blended. Shape into four patties and then lightly press both sides of each patty into the bread crumbs. Spray a baking pan with nonstick cooking spray and lay the patties gently in the pan. Spray the tops of the patties with the nonstick cooking spray and bake at 350 degrees for 25 to 30 minutes until patties are slightly golden brown. Serve plain or with your favorite fruit-sweetened ketchup.

These patties are good in a sandwich with sliced tomato and lettuce. My husband does not enjoy plain spinach like Popeye the make-believe character does! That is one reason I try to find ways to disguise the spinach so that he will eat it. For myself, I love fresh spinach with fresh lemon juice and a sprinkle of salt—mmm good! But for all you moms and dads who are trying to find a way to help your kids or yourselves to eat more green veggies, try these delicious breaded potato spinach patties and enjoy! —Linda

Yield: 4 patties

(Per patty) Calories: 122   Total Fat: 5.7g   Saturated Fat: 0.9g   Sodium: 196.2mg   Total Carbohydrates: 15.8mg   Fiber: 2.2g   Protein: 2.5g

Red Pepper Fritters

Mix all the ingredients together except for the canola oil. Put oil in a medium-hot skillet and spoon 1/4 cup of batter into the pan for each fritter. Fry until golden brown on both sides of the fritter. Serve hot!

These are great with Tofutti Sour Supreme, guacamole, and mild salsa spooned on top of each fritter. Serve the fritters with Spanish rice and a taco salad. We love to share these simple but special meals with our friends. Food always seems to taste better when shared with others. Enjoy! —Linda

1 cup corn, fresh or frozen

1/4 cup plain soymilk

1/4 cup white wheat flour

1/2 teaspoon All-Purpose Veggie Salt

1/4 teaspoon sea salt

2 tablespoons minced sweet red pepper

1 tablespoon minced green onions, steamed

1 tablespoon canola oil

Tofutti Sour Supreme for topping, optional

Guacamole, for topping, optional

Mild salsa, for topping, optional

Yield: 6 fritters

(Per fritter) Calories: 70   Total Fat: 2.7g   Saturated Fat: 0.2g   Sodium: 146.0mg   Total Carbohydrates: 11.4mg   Fiber: 0.9g   Protein: 1.0g

Fast & Easy

Vegetable
Chop Suey
p. 109

Southwestern
Chili Boats
p. 112

Stuffing Tarts
p. 110

South Pacific
Shish Kebabs
p. 108

Mushroom
Florentine Pastries
p. 111

Chicken Ratatouille

1 tablespoon extra virgin olive oil

1 medium onion, diced

2 cups peeled, diced eggplant

1/2 cup slivered yellow bell pepper

2 cloves garlic, minced

2 cups canned diced tomatoes

2 teaspoons sugar

1 teaspoon Italian seasoning

1/4 teaspoon thyme

1/4 teaspoon Vegetarian Express Pepper-Like Seasoning

1/4 teaspoon onion powder

Pinch cayenne pepper

Salt to taste

1 tablespoon soy margarine

1 cup Morningstar Farms Meal Starters Chik'n Strips or meat substitute of your choice

4 potatoes, baked, ready to serve

Soy sour cream

In a medium saucepan, heat olive oil and sauté onion until translucent. Add eggplant, garlic, and bell pepper. Cook until eggplant is tender. Add tomatoes, sugar, Italian seasoning, thyme, Pepper-Like Seasoning, onion powder, cayenne pepper, and salt, and simmer for 30 minutes. In a separate frying pan, sauté Chik'n Strips in margarine until golden and slightly crispy on edges. Add to sauce mixture and simmer for another 5 minutes. Serve over baked potatoes that have been slit down the middle and opened wide enough to make room to spoon in the ratatouille. Top off with a dollop of soy sour cream.

I like this dish a little spicy, but if you like to kick it up a notch, add 1 teaspoon crushed red pepper flakes when you add the rest of the seasonings. Actually, this is my favorite way to make it! Sometimes I serve it over brown rice or pasta instead of the potatoes. Either way, it's delicious! —Brenda

Yield: 4 1-cup servings

(Per serving with potato) Calories: 298   Total Fat: 7.0g   Saturated Fat: 1.6g   Sodium: 178.8mg   Total Carbohydrates: 52.9mg   Fiber: 8.1g   Protein: 9.3g

Tomato Spinach Soup

Heat olive oil in a medium saucepan. Sauté onion and garlic until onion is clear. Add the rest of the ingredients and cook over medium heat for 5 to 10 minutes or until hot. Stir frequently to avoid burning. Serve hot with a dollop of soy sour cream and a sprinkle of chives.

This soup is great when you are tired and don't feel like cooking much. You can substitute dried basil if you cannot get the fresh. However, the fresh adds tons more flavor. —Cinda

1 tablespoon extra virgin olive oil

1/2 cup chopped sweet onion

1 teaspoon minced garlic

1 cup plain soymilk

1 15-ounce can tomato sauce

1 14.5-ounce can diced tomatoes in sauce

2 teaspoons sugar

2 cups chopped fresh spinach

1 cup frozen shelled edamame

1/4 cup chopped fresh basil

1/2 teaspoon salt

1 tablespoon Saucy Ranch Seasoning

Soy sour cream

Chopped chives

Yield: 4 1-cup servings

(Per serving) Calories: 219.8   Total Fat: 8.5g   Saturated Fat: 1.0g   Sodium: 372.1mg   Total Carbohydrates: 27.0mg   Fiber: 6.6g   Protein: 12.0g

Barley Rice Chili

2 cups water

1/2 cup tomato juice

1/2 cup canned diced tomatoes

1/2 cup mild salsa

1/2 cup diced onions

1/2 teaspoon Saucy Ranch Seasoning

1 teaspoon All-Purpose Veggie Salt

1/2 cup canned kidney beans, drained

1/2 cup canned black beans, drained

1/2 cup canned great northern beans, drained

1/4 cup frozen corn

1/4 cup uncooked instant brown rice

1/4 cup uncooked quick barley

Fresh parsley (optional)

4 tablespoons Tofutti Sour Supreme (optional)

Add all ingredients except the parsley and Tofutti Sour Supreme to a medium-sized pan and bring to a boil. Cook at a slow boil approximately 10 minutes. Turn the soup down and let it simmer another 10 minutes. Garnish with fresh parsley and Tofutti Sour Supreme. Serve with your favorite salad and whole wheat bread.

This quick-to-prepare soup is really good and nutritious. I think it is even better when it is made the day before because the flavors have had time to blend. There is nothing like coming home to the smells of homemade soup and bread! The memory of those special times still makes me feel warm and loved. Soup—something so simple, yet its fragrance is so lasting! —Linda

Yield: 4 1-cup servings

(Per serving) Calories: 204   Total Fat: 0.9g   Saturated Fat: 0.2g   Sodium: 300.5mg   Total Carbohydrates: 41.3mg   Fiber: 8.0g   Protein: 9.0g

Safari No-Bake Beans

Put onions in a glass bowl with olive oil and place a glass lid on top. Microwave onions until they are clear in color. Put cooked onions in a skillet and add fresh garlic, curry powder, salt, and onion powder. Cook 2 to 3 minutes and then add beans, tomato sauce, ketchup, and water. Stir until everything is well mixed. Let the bean mixture simmer for approximately 5 to 10 minutes. Serve hot or cold.

When my sisters and I and our friend Sandy Miller were in South Africa, we had the privilege of staying in the home of Dané Venter and her mother Derika. They served us baked beans for breakfast with fresh bread and rolls. They also had a beautiful tray of grapes, avocados, fresh fruits, and sliced tomatoes. We were so blessed by the hospitality and warmth of their home. They made us feel like it was our home too. These delicious beans are even better when made the day before because the flavors have a chance to blend more. I hope you enjoy these no-bake beans as much as I did! —Linda

1/4 cup minced onions

1/2 teaspoon minced fresh garlic

1 tablespoon extra virgin olive oil

3/4 teaspoon curry powder

1/2 teaspoon sea salt

1/2 teaspoon onion powder

2 1/2 cups canned navy beans, drained and rinsed

3 1/2 cups tomato sauce

1/4 cup fruit-sweetened ketchup

1/2 cup water

Yield: 6 1/2-cup servings

(Per serving) Calories: 194   Total Fat: 3.1g   Saturated Fat: 0.4g   Sodium: 174.9mg   Total Carbohydrates: 34.1mg   Fiber: 10.4g   Protein: 8.4g

Pesto Pomodoro Pasta

2 cups whole wheat penne

1 cup diced fresh tomatoes

2 tablespoons Florentine pesto (recipe below)

2 tablespoons pasta water

FLORENTINE PESTO

1/2 cup extra virgin olive oil

1 cup chopped fresh spinach

2 cups chopped fresh basil

1/2 cup pine nuts

1/2 teaspoon salt

1 teaspoon minced fresh garlic

In a medium saucepan, cook pasta according to package directions. Drain, reserving 2 tablespoons of the liquid. In a serving bowl, combine Florentine pesto, fresh tomatoes, hot pasta, and reserved liquid. Gently stir to combine and serve.

This sounds really easy and basic, but like I learned while in Italy, some of the best foods are just that! If you are using pesto that you have made and frozen, just defrost it in the microwave or in a small saucepan on the stove. —Cinda

For pesto: Place all ingredients in a food processor or blender and process until smooth.

I fell in love with pesto while traveling throughout Italy with my family. The different ways they serve it are creative and endless. I added fresh spinach to my recipe for extra nutrition. You can use walnuts if you do not have pine nuts. Fresh ingredients are a must. I like to make extra pesto and then freeze it in ice cube trays. This makes it quick and easy to add to your recipes as you need it. —Cinda

Yield: 4 1-cup servings; 4 1/4-cup pesto servings

(Per serving recipe) Calories: 263 Total Fat: 6.4g Saturated Fat: 1.0g Sodium: 32.6mg Total Carbohydrates: 40.2mg Fiber: 6.7g Protein: 10.8g

(Per serving pesto) Calories: 361 Total Fat: 38.7g Saturated Fat: 4.5g Sodium: 243.0mg Total Carbohydrates: 3.6mg Fiber: 1.6g Protein: 3.1g

Portobello Mushroom Penne

Melt margarine in a large frying pan over medium heat. Sauté onion until clear. Add mushrooms, garlic, dried thyme, parsley, and salt. Cook until mushrooms are tender. Mix cornstarch with vegetable stock and add to mushrooms. Simmer several minutes. Add nondairy creamer. Simmer 1 to 2 minutes more and pour over cooked pasta. Toss and serve hot! Garnish with fresh thyme.

The taste of the broth and the mushrooms really wakes up your taste buds! I love mushrooms and have used a combination of other mushrooms with this recipe! Some of the wild mushrooms can give it a heavy, earthy taste, so add sparingly. If you like a little more broth, then reduce the pasta to 3 cups. I love the minipenne with this dish; angel hair is also a favorite, but you can use any pasta of your choice. Brown rice complements this dish as well, so you have lots of options! —Brenda

2 tablespoons soy margarine

1 medium onion, cut into small slivers

4 cups cubed portobello mushrooms

1 cup sliced white mushrooms

2 cloves garlic, minced

1 teaspoon dried thyme leaves

1 teaspoon parsley

1 teaspoon salt

1 tablespoon cornstarch

1 1/2 cups vegetable stock

1/2 cup Silk brand creamer

4 cups cooked minipenne pasta

Fresh thyme leaves

Yield: 4 1-cup servings

(Per serving) Calories: 291 Total Fat: 6.7g Saturated Fat: 1.7g Sodium: 611.3mg Total Carbohydrates: 46.2mg Fiber: 9.1g Protein: 14.9g

Pasta Puttanesca

1 tablespoon extra virgin olive oil

2 teaspoons minced fresh garlic

2 cups diced fresh tomatoes

1 tablespoon fresh minced oregano leaves

1/2 cup sliced Italian black olives

Salt to taste

Four servings of your favorite pasta

Heat olive oil in a medium saucepan. Sauté fresh garlic in oil for 2 minutes. Add the rest of the ingredients and simmer for 10 to 15 minutes. While topping is simmering, cook 4 servings of your favorite pasta according to package directions. Serve hot.

It doesn't get much easier than this! And your family will think you cooked all day! Italian black olives have a strong pungent flavor and are quite delicious. However, you can use regular black olives. If you want to lower your sodium intake, soak ripe olives for 2 minutes in cold water; drain and then add to dish. Surprisingly enough, this quick step reduces sodium by 5 to 6 percent. Garden fresh tomatoes are the best for this dish. I get them from my husband Joel's garden. If you don't have a garden (and you don't live near us), try to find a farmers' market in your area. It will be worth your trouble. —Cinda

Yield: 4 servings

(Per serving) Calories: 69 Total Fat: 5.3g Saturated Fat: 0.7g Sodium: 151.1mg Total Carbohydrates: 5.2mg Fiber: 1.9g Protein: 1.0g

Edamame Fried Rice

Place shredded carrots in small bowl, cover, and microwave for 1 1/2 minutes. Set aside. Heat oil in skillet over medium heat. Sauté green onions in oil until clear. Increase heat and add celery, red bell pepper, mushrooms and carrots. When celery is crunchy but tender, add rice, cooked edamame, and soy sauce. Mix well and serve on a platter. Garnish with cashews.

I love to eat edamame like popcorn, but there are also so many recipes that are enhanced by these delicious beans! Sometimes for added flavor, right before serving, I drizzle 1 tablespoon dark sesame oil over the top of this fried rice and that gives it a whole different fabulous flavor! Stir-fry dishes definitely make cooking easy. From start to finish this recipe takes less than 30 minutes! Now that is what I call "fast and easy"! —Brenda

1/2 cup shredded carrots

1 tablespoon peanut oil

2 tablespoons minced green onions

1/2 cup minced celery

1/2 cup finely diced red bell pepper

1/2 cup chopped mushrooms

1 cup shelled, cooked edamame

2 cups cooked brown rice

2 tablespoons vegan soy sauce or Bragg Liquid Aminos

1/4 cup cashews

Yield: 10 1/2-cup servings

(Per serving) Calories: 326   Total Fat: 14.9g   Saturated Fat: 2.4g   Sodium: 383.8mg   Total Carbohydrates: 34.2mg   Fiber: 6.1g   Protein: 17.7g

South Pacific Shish Kebabs

4 long shish kebab sticks

1 small zucchini cut into 8 pieces

1 yellow squash cut into 8 pieces

4 baby portobello or button mushrooms

1 small eggplant, peeled and cut into cubes

8 pieces of pineapple, fresh or canned

8 pieces of red bell pepper

8 pieces of homemade gluten or your favorite canned gluten

1 cup of your favorite teriyaki sauce

2 cups cooked brown, wild, or saffron-flavored rice

Preheat oven to 425 degrees. Onto each shish kebab, stick 2 zucchini pieces, 2 yellow squash pieces, 1 mushroom, 2 pieces of pineapple, 2 pieces of red pepper, 2 pieces of gluten, and as many pieces of eggplant as will fit on the stick. (You can put the vegetables and gluten in any order you like. If you mix them up, it will look nicer when you serve them.) Spray a baking sheet with nonstick cooking spray. Place shish kebabs on the baking sheet and drizzle with teriyaki sauce. Bake for 15 to 20 minutes until vegetables are tender and slightly browned. You can also grill these shish kebabs. Serve on top of rice.

These are delicious and beautiful! You can also add grape tomatoes and pieces of sweet onion if you like. More or less vegetables may be needed depending on the size of your shish kebab sticks. I use 12-inch sticks. —Cinda

Yield: 4 shish kebabs and rice servings

(Per serving) Calories: 245   Total Fat: 1.7g   Saturated Fat: 0.3g   Sodium: 1301.2mg   Total Carbohydrates: 49.5mg   Fiber: 7.6g   Protein: 11.4g

Vegetable Chop Suey

In a medium-sized pan, put the vegetables, onions, Liquid Aminos, beef seasoning, and hot water. Cook for 10 minutes until vegetables are tender. Mix cornstarch and cold water together and stir into hot, bubbling vegetables. Continue stirring until mixture thickens. Serve over hot brown rice.

My husband and I love the simple things of life. We enjoy nature walks, picnics, reading out loud to each other, and sitting on our front porch in the evening listening to all the night sounds. We have found that the simple, inexpensive things in life that God has provided bring the most joy. This Vegetable Chop Suey is one of those simple meals that we enjoy together. I serve this dish with a colorful vegetable tray. —Linda

2 cups frozen stir-fry vegetables

1/2 cup slivered onions

2 tablespoons Bragg Liquid Aminos

1 tablespoon McKay's Beef Seasoning (Vegan Special)

2 cups hot water

1/4 cup cornstarch

1/4 cup cold water

4 cups hot cooked brown rice

Yield: 4 1-cup servings

(Per serving) Calories: 406   Total Fat: 2.95g   Saturated Fat: 0.58g   Sodium: 912.50mg   Total Carbohydrates: 85.18mg   Fiber: 12.86g   Protein: 12.74g

Stuffing Tarts

1/4 cup extra virgin olive oil or soy margarine

1/2 cup chopped onion

3/4 cup chopped celery

1/2 cup chopped fresh mushrooms

3 cups herb-seasoned stuffing mix

1 cup water

1 tablespoon McKay's Chicken Seasoning (Vegan Special)

4 slices vegetarian turkey

Your favorite gravy

Heat oil or melt margarine in a skillet over medium heat. Sauté onion, celery, and mushrooms until onion is clear. In a medium bowl, stir cooked vegetables into stuffing mix. Mix vegetarian chicken seasoning into water and pour over bread crumb mixture. Stir until well mixed and moistened, set aside. Spray your muffin tins with nonstick cooking spray. Gently place a slice of vegetarian turkey into the bottom of each muffin cup. Spoon the stuffing on top. Bake at 350 degrees for about 15 minutes or until stuffing is golden brown on top. Serve hot with your favorite gravy.

This is my favorite way to serve stuffing! It is elegant, easy, and delicious. If the stuffing is too dry when you are mixing it, then add a little more of the soy margarine. You can also make these ahead of time and freeze right in the muffin pan. Just let them defrost before you bake them. My kids love the leftovers the next day—that is, if there are any! —Cinda

Yield: 4 tartlets

(Per tartlet) Calories: 329   Total Fat: 18.1g   Saturated Fat: 2.3g   Sodium: 1264.4mg   Total Carbohydrates: 34.3mg   Fiber: 3.8g   Protein: 9.9g

Mushroom Florentine Pastries

Bake pastry shells according to package directions. While shells are baking, melt margarine in a large skillet over medium heat. Sauté onions until translucent. Add mushrooms and fresh spinach. Continue to cook until spinach is wilted. Drain excess juice from skillet. Mix together soymilk, Wondra flour, and onion powder until smooth, then add to spinach mixture, stirring constantly. Continue cooking on medium heat until thickened and bubbly. Remove from heat and salt to taste. Pour mixture into baked puff pastry shells. Serve hot!

I love potpies mostly because of the pastry! Using the puff pastry shells cuts the time and work in half! You can find puff pastry shells in the freezer section of your grocery store. This is such an elegant entrée, yet only 30 minutes or less to make! Add a nice green salad and that's all you need for dinner! Your family will think you cooked all day! —Brenda

4 puff pastry shells

2 tablespoons soy margarine

1 medium onion, minced

3 cups sliced mushrooms

6 cups washed and drained fresh baby spinach

1/2 teaspoon onion powder

Salt to taste

3 cups soymilk

1/2 cup Wondra flour or very fine all-purpose flour

Yield: 4 pastries

(Per serving - filling) Calories: 179 Total Fat: 7.4g Saturated Fat: 2.1g Sodium: 177.4mg Total Carbohydrates: 24.6mg Fiber: 2.5g Protein: 7.0g

Southwestern Chili Boats

2 medium potatoes

2 tablespoons +
   2 teaspoons Tofutti
   Sour Supreme

1/8 teaspoon sea salt

1/4 teaspoon Saucy Ranch
   Seasoning

2 tablespoons water

1/2 cup chili beans

Olives (optional)

2 teaspoons fresh chives
   (optional)

Scrub potatoes and poke them almost all the way through in several places to keep them from exploding in the microwave. Put whole potatoes in a glass dish with a lid and microwave for 5 to 6 minutes. (You can also bake them in the oven—just allow more time.) When potatoes are done, carefully pull the skin off the top only. Scoop out hot potatoes into a mixing bowl leaving about 1/4 inch of the potatoes in the skin all the way around. This will make your potato boats sturdy.

Mix Tofutti Sour Supreme, salt, water, and Saucy Ranch Seasoning with the potatoes. Stir until well mixed. Put 1/2 cup of seasoned potatoes in each boat, pressing the filling up the sides while leaving a well in the middle of the boat. Heat chili beans and put 1/4 cup of beans in the middle of the boat. Spoon 1 teaspoon of Tofutti Sour Supreme on top. Garnish with chives and olives.

My husband also likes these potatoes filled with baked beans instead of the chili beans. Or you can use a broccoli-veggie cheese sauce for filling. These potatoes can also be made the night before and then warmed in the microwave. They not only look appetizing, but they are delicious! Enjoy!
—Linda

Yield: 2 chili boats

(Per chili boat) Calories: 254 Total Fat: 3.2g Saturated Fat: 1.0g Sodium: 303.0mg Total Carbohydrates: 49.0mg Fiber: 7.6g Protein: 8.1g

Vegetable Burritos

Heat olive oil in a skillet over medium heat. Sauté onion until translucent. Add celery, pimentos, zucchini, and yellow squash. When almost tender add broccoli florets, seasoning, and water. Let simmer until vegetables are tender but not wilted. Set aside. In a nonstick skillet on medium-high heat, place tortillas and flip back and forth until heated throughout. Spoon 1/2 cup brown rice into center of tortilla. Layer vegetables on top. Use any of the optional toppings or omit as desired. Fold bottom of tortilla up towards center, then fold each side over. Serve hot!

I love vegetables just about any way you can fix them. Sometimes though, when I am in a hurry, I don't have time to fix a complete meal. This is one way to get a good variety of vegetables and do it in a hurry. Best of all, it's delicious! I love to add mild hot sauce and guacamole to mine. —Brenda

2 tablespoons extra virgin olive oil

1 medium onion, cut into small slivers

1 cup small pieces of diagonally sliced celery

1/2 cup roasted, sliced pimentos

1 cup 1/8-inch thick half circles of zucchini

1 cup 1/8-inch thick half circles of yellow squash

1 cup broccoli florets

2 tablespoons taco seasoning mix

1 cup water

Salt to taste

4 10-inch whole wheat flour tortillas

2 cups cooked brown rice

1/2 cup hot sauce (optional)

1 cup guacamole (optional)

1/2 cup Tofutti Sour Supreme (optional)

Yield: 4 10–inch burritos

(Per serving - filling) Calories: 218   Total Fat: 7.9g   Saturated Fat: 1.1g   Sodium: 729.9mg   Total Carbohydrates: 32.2mg   Fiber: 3.6g   Protein: 4.4g

Mexican Lasagna

2 cups refried beans

1 cup water

12 corn tortillas, cut into
four triangle-shaped
pieces each

1 1/2 cups mild picante
sauce

1/2 cup diced green chiles

1/2 cup sliced black olives

1 cup cooked brown rice

1/4 cup minced scallions

2 tablespoons minced
jalapeño peppers
(optional)

1 cup crushed tortilla
chips

1 cup shredded lettuce

1 cup fresh diced tomatoes

Side dish of guacamole

Side dish of hot sauce of
your choice

Preheat oven to 400 degrees. Mix together refried beans and water. Set aside. In a 9-inch deep glass pie plate, layer ingredients in this order: one third of the refried beans, tortilla triangles (don't overlap them, but do cover the beans each time), picante sauce, green chiles, black olives, rice, scallions, and jalapeño peppers if using. Repeat layers ending with refried beans and jalapeño peppers if using. Cover with aluminum foil and bake for 30 minutes or until hot and bubbly. Remove from oven and add crushed tortilla chips, lettuce, and tomatoes. Serve with a side of guacamole and hot sauce!

I love Mexican food and this recipe gives you all your typical Mexican flavors in one dish! You can make it the night before and bake it 30 minutes before you are ready to serve. I love the taste of jalapeño peppers, but leave them out if you don't like the heat! This is a complete meal in itself without adding a thing! Fast, easy, and yummy! —Brenda

Yield: 6 slices

(Per slice) Calories: 350 Total Fat: 6.0g Saturated Fat: 0.9g Sodium: 479.6mg Total Carbohydrates: 60.2mg Fiber: 9.9g Protein: 10.0g

Desserts

Blueberry
Cheesecake
p. 125

Tangy Citrus
Parfait
p. 135

Lemon Poppy Seed
Minicakes
p. 127

Pumpkin Cake
p. 129

Georgia Peach
Shortcake
p. 131

Apricot Oatmeal Cookies

3/4 cup sugar

1/3 cup soy margarine

1/2 teaspoon pure vanilla extract

1 tablespoon cornstarch

2 tablespoons water

1/2 cup whole wheat pastry flour

1/2 teaspoon Rumford Baking Powder

1/4 teaspoon salt

1 1/4 cups dry quick oats

1/2 cup coarsely chopped walnuts

1/2 cup minced dried apricots

Heat oven to 350 degrees. In a large mixing bowl, combine sugar, margarine, pure vanilla extract, and water. Cream together and then add the rest of the ingredients. Drop dough by rounded tablespoons about 2 inches apart onto an ungreased cookie sheet. Flatten slightly with the palm of your hand or a spatula. Bake 10 to 14 minutes or until golden brown. Cool slightly then remove from cookie sheet.

These are soft, chewy, and delicious. Keep fresh by storing in an airtight plastic container. You can also freeze them for 1 to 2 months in a freezer-safe container. For variety, try adding raisins, dried cranberries, prunes, or dates. You can also substitute pecans or your favorite nut for the walnuts. —Brenda

Yield: 15 cookies

(Per cookie) Calories: 164   Total Fat: 7.0g   Saturated Fat: 1.7g   Sodium: 90.5mg   Total Carbohydrates: 24.5mg   Fiber: 2.3g   Protein: 2.1g

Cinnamon Catie-Doodles

Preheat oven to 350 degrees. In a medium mixing bowl, beat margarine and 3/4 cup sugar with an electric mixer until fluffy. Beat in soymilk and pure vanilla extract until well blended. Add flour, cornstarch, and baking powder, mixing dough until smooth. Place in refrigerator and chill for 15 minutes. Combine cinnamon and 2/3 cup sugar in a small bowl and set aside. Shape dough into 2-inch balls and roll in cinnamon-sugar mixture until well coated. Place 2 inches apart on a baking sheet that has been sprayed with nonstick cooking spray. Bake for 10 to 12 minutes until lightly browned on the bottom. Transfer to a wire rack to cool. Cookies will be very soft but will firm up when cooled.

My daughter Catie loves snickerdoodle cookies, so I asked her to make some that do not have any dairy products in them. She immediately went to work, and soon our house was filled with the wonderful smells of cinnamon and vanilla. She said that they do not spread out as much as those with dairy when they are baking, but they definitely taste wonderful! —Cinda

- 1 3/4 cups unbleached all-purpose flour
- 1/4 cup cornstarch
- 1 teaspoon baking powder
- 1/2 cup margarine, softened
- 3/4 cup + 2/3 cup granulated sugar
- 1/4 cup vanilla soymilk
- 1 1/2 teaspoons pure vanilla extract
- 4 tablespoons ground cinnamon

Yield: 24 cookies

(Per cookie) Calories: 118 Total Fat: 3.8g Saturated Fat: 1.4g Sodium: 58.0mg Total Carbohydrates: 20.6mg Fiber: 0.9g Protein: 1.0g

Peanut Butter Bars

1 1/2 cups unbleached
    all-purpose flour

1 teaspoon baking powder

1 teaspoon baking soda

1 cup packed brown sugar

2 tablespoons cornstarch

1/2 cup peanut butter

1/4 cup canola oil

1/4 cup soymilk

1 teaspoon pure vanilla
    extract

1/2 cup coarsely chopped
    peanuts

In a medium-sized mixing bowl, place all dry ingredients and stir to mix well. Make a well in the center of the dry ingredients, and add peanut butter, canola oil, soymilk, pure vanilla extract, and chopped peanuts. Stir until well combined. Spray an 8 x 8-inch baking dish with nonstick cooking spray. Pour batter into prepared pan and spread evenly. Bake in a 350-degree oven for 25 to 30 minutes until a knife, when inserted in the middle, comes out clean. Remove from oven and cool completely. When cool, cut into 12 bars.

Peanuts are my absolute favorite of all the nuts! So it would only be right for me to create a recipe with them as the main ingredient. These bars are easy to make and delicious. They freeze well, so you might just want to make a double batch. —Cinda

Yield: 12 bars

(Per bar) Calories: 335   Total Fat: 18.4g   Saturated Fat: 3.1g   Sodium: 150.9mg   Total Carbohydrates: 36.5mg   Fiber: 2.3g   Protein: 8.5g

Pumpkin Pie Squares

Place all ingredients in a medium-sized mixing bowl and stir until thoroughly combined. Pour over crust and bake in a 425-degree oven for 15 minutes. Reduce oven temperature to 350 degrees and continue baking for 40 minutes. Remove from oven and cool on rack for 15 to 20 minutes before cutting into squares. Store in refrigerator. Squares will be firm when completely cooled.

For crust: Combine cookie crumbs, sugar, and margarine, and stir until well mixed. Press in a 9 x 13-inch baking dish that has been sprayed with nonstick cooking spray.

I love just about anything with pumpkin! This is easy to make and a nice twist on the traditional pie. You can serve with a dollop of a nondairy whipped topping and a sprinkle of cinnamon. —Cinda

Cookie crust
(recipe below)

3 3/4 cups canned
pumpkin

1 cup plain soymilk

1/4 cup cornstarch

1/4 cup soy margarine,
melted

1/2 cup honey

1/2 cup pure maple syrup

1 teaspoon pure vanilla
extract

3 teaspoons ground
cinnamon

1/2 teaspoon allspice

1/4 teaspoon ginger

1 tablespoon molasses

1/4 teaspoon salt

Nondairy whipped cream
(optional)

COOKIE CRUST

2 cups ginger cookie
crumbs

1/4 cup sugar

4 tablespoons soy
margarine, melted

Yield: 15 squares

(Per square) Calories: 240 Total Fat: 7.9g Saturated Fat: 2.8g Sodium: 142.4mg Total Carbohydrates: 43.5mg Fiber: 2.1g Protein: 1.0g

(Per serving - crust only) Calories: 96 Total Fat: 4.7g Saturated Fat: 1.6g Sodium: 66.3mg Total Carbohydrates: 13.5mg Fiber: 0g Protein: 0g

Blackberry Tarts

1/2 cup raw quick oats

1/2 cup whole wheat pastry flour

1/4 teaspoon sea salt

2 tablespoons soy margarine, melted

1 tablespoon pure maple syrup

4 tablespoons fruit-sweetened blackberry jam

In a medium-sized bowl, mix oats, flour, and salt together. Add margarine, and maple syrup, working it into dry ingredients with a fork. Mix until well blended. Spray 6 individual 3-inch sections of a muffin pan with nonstick cooking spray. Set aside 2 tablespoons of the dry mixture for topping. Divide remaining dry mixture equally into each section. Press mixture into the bottom and sides of each muffin section.

Put 2 teaspoons of blackberry jam in each muffin section and then sprinkle 1 teaspoon of dry mixture on top. Bake at 350 degrees for about 15 minutes until crust is golden brown. Take out of the oven, run a knife around each tart, and let them sit a couple of minutes. Put the knife under each tart, gently lift it out, and set it on a plate to cool.

These minitarts are so much fun to make. Experiment with different kinds of jam or homemade fillings. They are also are good for lunches and picnics. I love to make extra and share them with my friends. —Linda

Yield: 10 minitarts

(Per minitart) Calories: 78.3 Total Fat: 2.6g Saturated Fat: 0.9g Sodium: 71.2mg Total Carbohydrates: 12.7mg Fiber: 1.2g Protein: 1.1g

Key Lime Pie

Preheat oven to 350 degrees. In a 9-inch glass pie plate, combine graham cracker crumbs, sugar, and margarine. Mix well and then press all around, covering pie plate evenly. Bake at 350 degrees for 10 to 15 minutes. Remove from oven and set aside to cool.

Grate rind and squeeze the juice from 1 fresh lime, saving the pulp—the soft, fleshy part of the fruit. In a blender, mix Tofutti Better Than Cream Cheese; maple syrup; honey; pure vanilla extract; lime juice, pulp, and zest; cornstarch; nondairy creamer; and flour, and process until smooth and creamy. Pour into baked piecrust. Bake for 40 to 45 minutes. The pie filling should look slightly raised around the edges but have no change in color. Cool completely and then cover top completely with nondairy whipped topping. Refrigerate for 2 to 4 hours until completely cold. Garnish top with additional zest of lime.

I love the tangy citrus taste of this pie combined with the creamy texture of the nondairy topping. The combination is smooth, wonderful, and melts in your mouth! —Brenda

- 1 1/2 cups graham cracker crumbs
- 3 tablespoons sugar
- 5 tablespoons soy margarine, melted
- 2 8-ounce containers Tofutti Better Than Cream Cheese
- 1/2 cup pure maple syrup
- 1/2 cup honey
- 1 teaspoon pure vanilla extract
- 1 medium lime, juice, pulp, and zest
- 3 tablespoons cornstarch
- 1/4 cup nondairy creamer
- 3 tablespoons whole wheat pastry flour
- Nondairy whipped topping

Yield: 12 slices

(Per slice) Calories: 313   Total Fat: 13.1g   Saturated Fat: 4.3g   Sodium: 305.9mg   Total Carbohydrates: 48.2mg   Fiber: 2.1g   Protein: 3.2g

Sweet Potato Pie

1 14-ounce package silken tofu

1 14-ounce package extra-firm tofu

3 cups baked, peeled, and mashed sweet potatoes

2 teaspoons cinnamon

1 teaspoon ginger

1/4 teaspoon cloves

1/2 teaspoon nutmeg

1 teaspoon salt

2 teaspoons pure vanilla extract

1 cup Florida Crystals

1/4 cup Silk brand creamer

1 premade or purchased frozen piecrust

Nondairy whipped topping (optional)

Preheat oven to 350 degrees. Blend all ingredients except the piecrust in a food processor until smooth and creamy. Pour into pie shell and bake for 1 to 1 1/2 hours until a toothpick inserted into the center comes out clean.

This is an old Southern favorite that tastes very similar to pumpkin pie. It is also good baked without the crust in individual custard baking dishes! For added dining pleasure, serve with a dollop of nondairy whipped topping! "Ya'll gonna luv it!" —Brenda

Yield: 8 slices

(Per slice) Calories: 308 Total Fat: 8.3g Saturated Fat: 1.2g Sodium: 405.1mg Total Carbohydrates: 52.2mg Fiber: 3.7g Protein: 8.4g

Blueberry Cheesecake

In a medium saucepan over medium heat, combine frozen blueberries, 1/2 cup granulated sugar, and 1/4 cup water. Continue heating. Stir slurry in to blueberries. Continue to cook, stirring occasionally, until mixture boils and thickens. Remove from heat and refrigerate. Cool completely.

Preheat oven to 350 degrees. In a 9-inch glass pie plate, combine graham cracker crumbs, granulated sugar, and margarine. Mix well and then press all around, covering pie plate evenly. Bake at 350 degrees for 10 to 15 minutes. Remove from oven and set aside to cool.

In a mixing bowl, combine Tofutti Better Than Cream Cheese and powdered sugar. Mix with electric mixer until smooth. Add nondairy whipped topping and blend on low speed until smooth. Pour into cooled crust. Place in freezer for 1 to 2 hours until set. Top with blueberry mixture. Serve cold.

For slurry: Combine 3 tablespoons cold water and cornstarch. Stir until smooth.

This was one of my favorite desserts that Mom made when I was little. Of course, back then, she used regular cream cheese. I was so excited when I first tried the Tofutti Better Than Cream Cheese and was surprised at how good the texture and flavor were! I had a hard time believing it wasn't the real thing! After reading the label several times, I embraced this product and now use it in many of my desserts, as well as entrées too! —Brenda

---

- 3 cups frozen blueberries
- 1/2 cup + 3 tablespoons granulated sugar
- 1/4 cup water
- Slurry (recipe below)
- 1 1/2 cups graham cracker crumbs
- 5 tablespoons soy margarine, melted
- 2 8-ounce containers Tofutti Better Than Cream Cheese
- 1 cup powdered sugar
- 1 cup nondairy whipped topping

SLURRY

- 3 tablespoons cold water
- 3 tablespoons cornstarch

Yield: 8 slices

(Per slice) Calories: 450 Total Fat: 20.7g Saturated Fat: 7.5g Sodium: 459.7mg Total Carbohydrates: 64.1mg Fiber: 4.0g Protein: 4.9g

Banana Pecan Cupcakes

1/2 cup chopped pecans

1 1/2 cups whole wheat
flour

1 teaspoon baking powder

1 teaspoon baking soda

1 teaspoon cinnamon

1/2 cup sugar

1 tablespoon cornstarch

2 tablespoons soy
margarine, melted

4 medium-sized ripe
bananas

1 teaspoon pure vanilla
extract

Glaze (see recipe below)

MUFFIN GLAZE

3/4 cup powdered sugar

1 tablespoon soy
margarine, melted

1 teaspoon pure vanilla
extract

1 tablespoon soymilk

Toast pecans until fragrant in a 350-degree oven, microwave, or in a small skillet on the stovetop. (This usually takes about 5 minutes depending on which method you use. You do need to watch them carefully so they do not burn.) Combine all dry ingredients in a medium-sized mixing bowl and stir well. In a small mixing bowl, mash the 4 bananas and mix in melted margarine and pure vanilla extract. Stir well. Add to dry ingredients and stir just until dry ingredients are moistened. Stir in pecans. Line muffin pan with paper liners or spray each muffin depression with nonstick cooking spray. Divide the batter evenly between the 12 muffin depressions. Bake at 350 degrees for approximately 25 minutes until knife comes out clean when inserted into the middle of muffin. Remove from oven and transfer to a cooling rack. Drizzle with glaze.

For glaze: Mix all ingredients together until smooth and a consistency that will drizzle from a spoon. You can add less or more of the soymilk as needed. Drizzle onto muffins.

These muffins are easy to make and delicious. You can also make an 8 1/2 x 4 1/2-inch loaf if you prefer. These muffins freeze well, so you can double the recipe to be prepared for those drop-in guests! —Cinda

Yield: 12 cupcakes; 12 heaping tablespoons glaze

(Per cupcake) Calories: 174 Total Fat: 5.7g Saturated Fat: 1.0g Sodium: 157.8mg Total Carbohydrates: 30.0mg Fiber: 3.4g Protein: 3.1g
(Per tablespoon glaze) Calories: 9 Total Fat: 1.0g Saturated Fat: 0.3g Sodium: 10.6mg Total Carbohydrates: 0.3mg Fiber: 0g Protein: 0g

Lemon Poppy Seed Minicakes

Preheat the oven to 350 degrees. Spray 4 minicake pans with nonstick cooking spray. (I use small bowls 5 1/2 inches in diameter by 2 inches high.) Grate rind and squeeze juice from one fresh lemon, saving the pulp—the soft, fleshy part of the fruit. Combine lemon juice, zest, and pulp with the nondairy creamer and set aside. Combine the flour, poppy seeds, baking soda, baking powder, and salt, and set aside.

With an electric mixer at medium speed, beat oil with honey, maple syrup, pure vanilla extract, and cornstarch until smooth. Reduce the speed of the electric mixer to low and beat in flour mixture 1/3 at a time, alternating with 1/3 of the lemon-creamer mixture at a time. Beat until smooth. Pour the batter evenly into the four prepared cake pans. Bake for 20 minutes or until cake springs back slightly when lightly touched with a fingertip. Let cool. Drizzle frosting over cakes, reserving about 1/3 of the frosting. Layer pecan halves in a decorative circular pattern completely covering top of cake. Drizzle lightly with remaining frosting.

For frosting: Mix 1 tablespoon lemon juice with powdered sugar until smooth and sugar dissolves.

These cakes are light, fluffy, and have a zesty lemon flavor! I must confess that I love the batter as much as the finished cake! Unfrosted, these cakes also freeze very well. I have a sweet tooth, so I love the extra-sweet zing of the lemon frosting but you can certainly omit this step and not compromise the taste! —Brenda

1 lemon, juice, pulp, and zest

2/3 cup Silk brand creamer

1 1/3 cups whole wheat pastry flour

1/2 cup unbleached all-purpose flour

1 teaspoon poppy seeds

1 1/2 teaspoons baking soda

1/2 teaspoon baking powder

1/2 teaspoon salt

1/3 cup canola oil

1/2 cup honey

1/2 cup pure maple syrup

1/2 teaspoon pure vanilla extract

1/4 cup cornstarch

Frosting (recipe below)

Pecan halves

FROSTING

1 tablespoon fresh lemon juice

1/2 cup powdered sugar

Yield: 4 frosted minicakes

(Per 1/2 minicake) Calories: 368 Total Fat: 10.9g Saturated Fat: 0.7g Sodium: 869.5mg Total Carbohydrates: 87.0mg Fiber: 2.9g Protein: 2.2g

Pineapple Carrot Cake

1 cup grated carrots

3/4 cup raisins

1/2 cup canned crushed
pineapple, drained,
reserving juice

1/2 cup pineapple juice

1/2 cup water

3/4 teaspoon cinnamon

3/4 teaspoon nutmeg

1/2 teaspoon cloves

1/4 cup honey

1/4 cup pure maple syrup

1/2 teaspoon salt

1 8-ounce container
Tofutti Better Than
Cream Cheese

1 cup powdered sugar

1 cup nondairy whipped
cream

1 1/2 cups whole wheat
pastry flour

1 teaspoon baking powder

1 teaspoon baking soda

1/2 cup soymilk

1 teaspoon pure vanilla
extract

1/2 cup + 1/4 cup coarsely
chopped pecans

Preheat oven to 350 degrees. Spray 9-inch round cake pan with nonstick cooking spray and set aside. In a medium saucepan, gently simmer carrots, raisins, pineapple, pineapple juice, water, cinnamon, nutmeg, and cloves for 5 to 6 minutes. Add honey, maple syrup, and salt, and simmer for another 2 to 3 minutes. Remove from heat. Set aside to cool.

Make frosting. In a mixing bowl, combine Tofutti Better Than Cream Cheese and powdered sugar. Mix with electric mixer until smooth and then add nondairy whipped topping. Mix on low speed approximately 1 minute until smooth. Refrigerate.

In a large bowl, combine flour, baking powder, and baking soda. Add cooled carrot-raisin mixture, soymilk, and pure vanilla extract. Mix well and then fold in 1/2 cup pecan pieces. Pour into a prepared cake pan and bake for 45 to 50 minutes until cake springs back when lightly touched. Remove from cake pan and place on cake platter. Let cool completely and then spread with refrigerated frosting. Sprinkle with 1/4 cup chopped pecans. Store covered in refrigerator.

This moist and flavor-filled cake is sure to be a pleaser. I love the smell of cinnamon, nutmeg, and cloves that floats through the house while this is baking! You may want to double the recipe to have an extra cake stored in your freezer. Make more frosting while the second cake thaws, and you have a quick dessert for unexpected guests. —Brenda

Yield: 12 slices

(Per slice) Calories: 272 Total Fat: 9.5g Saturated Fat: 2.5g Sodium: 342.8mg Total Carbohydrates: 45.7mg Fiber: 3.6g Protein: 3.6g

Pumpkin Cake

In a medium-sized mixing bowl, combine all ingredients and stir until well mixed. Spray an 8 x 8-inch pan with nonstick cooking spray. Spread batter evenly in pan and bake at 350 degrees for 25 minutes until a knife inserted into the center comes out clean. Remove from oven and drizzle with glaze.

For glaze: Mix all ingredients together in a small bowl and drizzle on hot Pumpkin Cake.

My son, David, quite often brings 10 to 15 of his college friends home for the weekend. They have become part of our family, which also makes them "official recipe judges." I create new recipes, and they taste them all and help Joel, David, and Catie decide if it gets put in our new Micheff sister's cookbook! This cake made the "must be put in the cookbook" rating from everyone! But, if you are making this recipe for 10 college boys, you better make them each a recipe of their own. —Cinda

3 tablespoons Grapeseed Oil Vegenaise

1/2 cup sugar

1 tablespoon cornstarch

1 cup canned pumpkin

1/3 cup canola oil

1 cup flour

1 teaspoon baking powder

1/2 teaspoon baking soda

2 tablespoons cinnamon

1/2 teaspoon nutmeg

1/4 teaspoon ground ginger

1/2 teaspoon ground cloves

1/4 teaspoon salt

Glaze (see recipe below)

GLAZE

2/3 cup powdered sugar

1/2 teaspoon pure almond extract

1 tablespoon water

Yield: 12 pieces

(Per serving cake) Calories: 158 Total Fat: 8.6g Saturated Fat: 0.9g Sodium: 146.8mg Total Carbohydrates: 19.5mg Fiber: 1.6g Protein: 1.4g
(Per serving glaze) Calories: 9.7 Total Fat: 0g Saturated Fat: 0g Sodium: 0mg Total Carbohydrates: 1.7mg Fiber: 0g Protein: 0g

Pineapple Upside-Down Minicakes

1/2 cup white whole wheat flour

3/4 teaspoon Rumford Baking Powder

1/8 teaspoon sea salt

1/4 cup pineapple juice

1/4 cup orange juice

1/2 teaspoon pure vanilla extract

1 1/2 teaspoons canola oil

4 pineapple rings

4 pecan halves

1/4 cup pure maple syrup

Mix the dry ingredients together and make a well in the middle. Add pineapple juice, orange juice, pure vanilla extract, and canola oil. Mix until well blended.

In a regular-sized muffin pan, spray 4 sections with nonstick cooking spray. Pour 1 tablespoon of pure maple syrup in each section. Place a pecan half in the middle of each muffin section. Make a cut in the 4 pineapple rings and overlap it a little so it fits in each of the sections. Divide the batter into the 4 sections and spoon on top of each pineapple. Add water to the empty muffin cups so that your pan doesn't warp or the muffins overcook. Bake at 350 degrees for 20 to 25 minutes until a toothpick inserted in the middle of the cake comes out clean. When cakes are done, put a plate over the top of the muffin pan and flip it over so that the pineapple is on top.

I love to surprise my family with special treats. My husband really enjoyed this tasty little cake. It is pretty when served on a plate and garnished with sliced strawberries on the side. —Linda

Yield: 4 minicakes

(Per minicake) Calories: 169 Total Fat: 1.9g Saturated Fat: 0.2g Sodium: 146.2mg Total Carbohydrates: 36.6mg Fiber: 0.9g Protein: 2.0g

Georgia Peach Shortcake

In a small saucepan, pour in white grape peach juice. Bring juice to a slow boil. Mix cornstarch and cold water together and stir into hot juice until it thickens and changes color. (It will turn white when the cornstarch is added but will cook back to the clear color of the juice.) Take thickened juice off of the burner. Add maple syrup and cinnamon and stir until blended. Cool sauce and pour over fresh uncooked peaches. Gently mix until sauce covers peaches. Serve over shortcake or biscuits and top with nondairy whipped topping.

When I serve fresh peach shortcake, it is sure to bring a sparkle to my husband's eyes. And I love making him happy! Georgia Peach Shortcake is a delicious and easy dessert to serve for a crowd as well. This recipe is also great over pancakes, waffles, or hot cereal and can also be used as a pie filling. Enjoy! —Linda

1 cup white grape peach juice

2 tablespoons cornstarch

1 tablespoon cold water

1 tablespoon pure maple syrup

Sprinkle of cinnamon

2 cups sliced fresh peaches, uncooked

Purchased or homemade biscuits or shortcake

Yield: 4 servings

(Per serving peaches) Calories: 99   Total Fat: 0.2g   Saturated Fat: 0g   Sodium: 4.5mg   Total Carbohydrates: 24.9mg   Fiber: 1.3g   Protein: 0.8g

Cranapple Crisp

3 cups cubed apples (pieces should be large)

1/2 cup apple juice concentrate

1/4 cup water

1/4 cup whole berry cranberry sauce

2 tablespoons whole wheat flour

1/4 cup unbleached white flour

2 tablespoons soy margarine

1/8 teaspoon sea salt

Put apples, water, and apple juice concentrate in a pan over medium heat and cook until tender. Add extra water if needed. When apples are cooked, add whole berry cranberry sauce and pour into a small baking dish. (I always add the cranberries after the apples are cooked so that the clear color of the apples is preserved; otherwise, the whole dessert turns pink!)

Mix margarine, flours, and salt together. Sprinkle mixture on top of the crisp. Bake at 350 degrees for 20 to 25 minutes until golden brown.

When my husband was growing up, hardly a meal went by that they didn't have some kind of dessert. His mother took great delight in pleasing her family. Now my mother-in-law lives with us, and I try to find healthy treats and desserts that she will enjoy. She loves apple desserts and really loved this one. I hope you will like it too! —Linda

Yield: 4 1/2-cup servings

(Per serving) Calories: 182   Total Fat: 5.8g   Saturated Fat: 2.0g   Sodium: 137.4mg   Total Carbohydrates: 33.2mg   Fiber: 3.1g   Protein: 0.9g

Blueberry Almost Ice Cream

Put all the ingredients in the blender and blend until smooth. Serve in glass dishes and garnish with fresh strawberries.

My husband loves this fast and refreshing dessert. I serve it to him for supper with a smile! This cool, nutritious dessert supplies the recommended amount of blueberries for the day. By eating 1/2 cup of blueberries daily, you can just about double the amount of antioxidants most Americans get in a day! God's amazing little blueberries have emerged as nature's number 1 source of antioxidants among fresh fruits and vegetables. So sit back, relax, and enjoy this delicious treat! —Linda

1 cup frozen blueberries

1/2 cup frozen pineapple chunks

1 teaspoon pure vanilla extract

1 tablespoon pure maple syrup

1/2 cup soymilk

Fresh strawberries for garnish

Yield: 5 1/4-cup servings

(Per serving) Calories: 47   Total Fat: 0.4g   Saturated Fat: 0.1g   Sodium: 13.6mg   Total Carbohydrates: 10.8mg   Fiber: 1.0g   Protein: 0.4g

Bananas Sanner

2 tablespoons soy margarine

1/2 cup pure maple syrup

1 teaspoon cinnamon

1 1/2 teaspoons pure vanilla extract

3/4 cup pecans

2 large bananas

Your favorite pancakes or waffles

Nondairy whipped topping

In a medium sauté pan over medium heat, melt margarine with pure maple syrup. Add cinnamon, pure vanilla extract, and pecans. Simmer for 2 to 3 minutes. Slice bananas and add to the pan. Cook for another 2 to 3 minutes. Serve warm over pancakes or waffles. Top with a dollop of nondairy whipped topping.

During one of our family trips, my husband ordered a dessert called Bananas Foster. He enjoyed it so much that I was determined to make it at home for him. I discovered that there are many different recipes for it. They all had 6 or more tablespoons of butter in them, and some even had liqueurs in them. I decided to invent a recipe that would be easy to prepare and healthier too. I serve it over whole wheat waffles instead of ice cream, and my husband loves it! Of course, you could put a scoop of nondairy ice cream on the waffle too!
—Cinda

Yield: 6 servings

(Per serving) Calories: 231   Total Fat: 12.7g   Saturated Fat: 2.2g   Sodium: 42.6mg   Total Carbohydrates: 30.5mg   Fiber: 2.6g   Protein: 1.6g

Tangy Citrus Parfait

Put tofu, lemon juice, orange juice concentrate, pure vanilla extract, mandarin oranges, and maple syrup in the blender and blend until smooth. In each of 4 small parfait glasses, put 1/8 of the blender mix, 1/8 of the fresh fruit, 1/8 of the granola, and then a second layer of blender mix, fruit, and granola. Top with a piece of fruit. Chill until cold.

This dessert can be made a couple of hours before it is served. It is bright, colorful, and delicious. Sometimes I layer more fruit in the parfait than the recipe calls for just because our family loves fresh fruit. For variety I sometimes omit the lemon and orange juice and put frozen strawberries or blueberries in it. Enjoy! —Linda

3/4 12.3-ounce package Mori-Nu Tofu

1 tablespoon fresh squeezed lemon juice

1 teaspoon orange juice concentrate

1 teaspoon pure vanilla extract

1/4 cup drained mandarin oranges

2 tablespoons pure maple syrup

1/2 cup granola

1/2 cup + 4 pieces fresh fruit, such as strawberries, raspberries, blueberries

Yield: 4 parfaits

(Per parfait) Calories: 136   Total Fat: 3.8g   Saturated Fat: 3.8g   Sodium: 8.9mg   Total Carbohydrates: 22.0mg   Fiber: 1.9g   Protein: 4.9g

Piña Colada

2 cups frozen pineapple chunks

2 tablespoons pure virgin coconut oil

3 tablespoons pure maple syrup

1/4 cup white grape peach juice

Orange slices for garnish

Fresh strawberries for garnish

Put pineapple, coconut oil, maple syrup, and juice in the blender and whiz until smooth. Garnish with a slice of fresh orange and a strawberry. Serve right away.

This quick and easy dessert is sure to please your sweet tooth. It is also refreshing on a hot summer day. If you want the Piña Colada thicker, add a little less juice. Enjoy! —Linda

Yield: 4 servings

(Per serving) Calories: 179   Total Fat: 7.0g   Saturated Fat: 6.5g   Sodium: 12.1mg   Total Carbohydrates: 29.6mg   Fiber: 1.0g   Protein: 0g

Granny's Fudge

Spread peanut butter around in a glass bowl. Put carob chips on top of peanut butter and cover with a glass lid. Make sure carob chips are only touching peanut butter or they will burn. Microwave for 40 seconds to 1 minute, depending on how hot the microwave is. Take out of microwave and stir peanut butter and carob chips together until well mixed. Add Tofutti Better Than Cream Cheese and maple syrup. Toast coconut in the oven or microwave until golden in color. Add coconut and almonds to the mixture. Stir until mixed. Spray the bottom of a small pan with nonstick cooking spray and pat the fudge into the bottom of the pan. Cut into pieces and place in the refrigerator until ready to serve. This fudge is best stored in the refrigerator.

- 1/4 cup natural crunchy peanut butter
- 1/2 cup malt-sweetened carob chips
- 3 tablespoons Tofutti Better Than Cream Cheese
- 1 tablespoon pure maple syrup
- 1/4 cup toasted coconut
- 1/4 cup sliced almonds

If you would like this fudge a little sweeter, use 2 tablespoons of pure maple syrup instead of one. Make sure the peanut butter is moist and creamy, or the recipe will not turn out as well. Some natural peanut butters are hard and dry so choose carefully. My husband said that Granny's Fudge is really good and he enjoys it, but he still remembers what "real" fudge is like! So Granny's Fudge is not fudge to him, just a delicious treat. He used to eat a whole pound of sugary fudge at a time, but he began to have some problems with his joints. He decided to give up sugary desserts and now enjoys some natural treats, and he's feeling so much better! I love how God works on our hearts to change our desires and gives us His! —Linda

Yield: 16 pieces

(Per piece) Calories: 125   Total Fat: 9.5g   Saturated Fat: 5.1g   Sodium: 20.1mg   Total Carbohydrates: 8.8mg   Fiber: 1.7g   Protein: 3.1g

Resources

DRESSLER'S is currently producing some of the finest dairy alternative beverages available on the market today. Their soymilk is tasty, wholesome, and made from natural ingredients. Dressler's also offers Soy Add-ums, a dried vegan meat substitute.

Web site: **www.dresslerfoods.com**
E-mail: info@dresslerfoods.com
Phone: 1-888-526-6330
Address: Dressler's LLC
184 Panorama Lane, Walla Walla, WA 99362

YVES VEGGIE CUISINE produces healthy vegetarian soy meat substitutes that are not only packed with good nutrition and flavor but are low in fat and calories! One of the things we love best is the texture and also that it doesn't have an overwhelming flavor. It takes on whatever flavor you give it and no aftertaste that is common with other products!

Web site: **www.yvesveggie.com**
Phone: 1-800-434-4246

COUNTRY LIFE NATURAL FOODS offers a line of natural, whole, and organic foods at reasonable prices. They carry most of the specialty items in this cookbook such as Mori-Nu Tofu, Mori-Nu Mates, McKay's Chicken and Beef Seasonings, Bragg Liquid Aminos, Vegex, Emes Kosher Gelatin, pure maple syrup, whole grains, herbs, spices, and more than 1,200 other natural items. They will ship directly to your house via UPS. Contact them and ask for their free catalog.

Web site: **www.clnf.org**
Phone: 1-800-456-7694

FOLLOW YOUR HEART is located in Canoga Park, California. They offer Grapeseed Oil Vegenaise and the original Vegenaise. In our opinion, this is the best nondairy mayonnaise on the market.

Web site: **www.followyourheart.com**
Phone: 1-818-347-9946

AMERICAN NATURAL AND SPECIALTY BRANDS makes Better Than Milk. This soymilk is one of our favorites. We have used it in a lot of our recipes.

E-mail: info@betterthanmilk.com
Phone: 1-800-227-2320

CREATIVE FOODS INC. offers a wide variety of gluten products as well as coffee substitutes.

Web site: **www.creativefoodsinc.com**
E-mail: sales@creativefoodsinc.com;
buenocoffee@yahoo.com
Phone message: 541-504-1463
(Yollie) cell: 541-788-3663
Address: Creative Foods Inc.
460 NE Hemlock Ave, Suite B,
Redmond, OR 97756

TOFUTTI BRANDS offers a variety of nondairy items that are soy based and casein-free. They offer Sour Supreme, Better Than Cream Cheese, American Soy-Cheese Slices, Mozzarella Soy-Cheese Slices, and much more.

Web site: **www.tofutti.com**
E-mail: Tofuttibrands@aol.com
Phone: 1-908-272-2400
Address: Tofutti Brands, Inc.
50 Jackson Drive, Cranford, NJ 07016

MCKAY'S SEASONING makes the chicken and beef seasonings we use in many of our recipes. Our mom cooked with them when we were little girls, and we still love their seasoning today! Their beef seasoning has recently changed and we like it even better than before! And they offer vegan and no MSG versions of their popular products.

Web site: **www.mckaysseasoning.com**,
Phone: 419-531-8963
Address: Dismat Corporation
336 North Westwood Ave., Toledo, OH 43607

THE VEGETARIAN EXPRESS offers a wide variety of seasonings as well as prepackaged products, such as cookie mixes, pasta mixes, gravies, waffles, etc. We've tried many of them, and they are excellent! Their oatmeal cookie mix is incredible, and we use many of their seasonings in our recipes, including All-Purpose Veggie Salt, La Chikky Seasoning, Saucy Ranch Seasoning, Roasted Garlic & Red Bell Pepper Zip, Lemony Dill Zest, Greek Isle Seasoning, and Pepper-Like Seasoning.

Web site: **www.thevegetarianexpress.com**
Phone: 734-355-3593
Address: The Vegetarian Express
P.O. Box 33, South Lyon, MI 48178

ISLAND SPICE has a variety of spices, and their All-Purpose Seasoning is used in some of our recipes.

Web site: **www.islandspice.com**
E-mail: lawrence_shadeed@hotmail.com
Phone: 786-208-2066
Address: Island Spice, 15270 SW 15th St.,
Miami, FL 33194

BEST BET COFFEE AND SPICE We use many of their spices which are ever so rich in flavor and so much fresher than the ones that sit for months on the grocery store shelf!

Web site: **www.bestbetcoffeeandspice.com**
Email: info@bestbetcoffeeandspice.com
Phone: 702-236-3280
Address: Best Bet Coffee and Spice
Box 20861, Las Vegas, NV 89112

VEGEX Brewer's yeast extract is distributed at various locations nationwide. If you do not have a convenient retail location for Vegex, you can order it directly.

Contact: Jeff Poth
Phone: 908-782-1480 ext. 251

ADVENTIST BOOK CENTER provides a wide variety of natural foods and meat substitutes such as Worthington Vegetarian Burger, Brewer's yeast flakes, seasonings, and immitation bacon bits. To locate a store near you, please visit the Web site.

Web site: **www.adventistbookcenter.com**
Phone: 800-765-6955

THREE ANGELS BROADCASTING NETWORK (3ABN) For more information on healthy living, check the 3ABN Web site. You can view vegan cooking programs and receive additional recipes on 3ABN Television or 3ABN Radio online 24 hours a day. They offer a number of programs on health and its benefits.

Web site: **www.3abn.org**
E-mail: mail@3abn.org
Phone: 618-627-4651
Address: P.O. Box 220, West Frankfort, IL 62896

THE NEWSTART LIFESTYLE PROGRAM will give you more information about healthy living.

Phone: 1-530-637-4111
Address: Weimar Institute Newstart Life Center
P.O. Box 486, Weimar, CA 95736

Time-saving Tips

KEEP A WELL-STOCKED PANTRY

To successfully put together meals in minutes, you need a well-stocked pantry, refrigerator, and freezer. In other words, keep on hand ingredients that are used often and can be combined easily for simple and delicious meals. Then all you need to do is shop for fresh ingredients as needed. Many who are just learning the joys of cooking often ask us what foods we stock in our pantries, refrigerators, and freezers. Below are some of our suggestions.

Basic Pantry Items:
Whole wheat flour—white, regular, pastry
Sugar, brown sugar
Pure maple syrup
Aluminum-free baking powder
Baking soda
Oats
Rice
Dried pastas
Canned and dried fruits, vegetables, beans
Peanut butter
Dried beans and lentils
Canned tomato sauces
Canned soups
Carob chips
Honey
Vegetable oil, olive oil
Nonstick cooking spray
Dried gluten products
Other food items that have a long shelf life
Of course, any serious cook will always have fresh potatoes stored in a cool, dark place.

Basic Seasonings:
Salt
Vegetarian chicken and beef seasonings
Dried parsley, basil, thyme, oregano, rosemary, dill, sage
Chili powder
Garlic powder
Onion powder

Cayenne pepper
Cumin
Minced onion
Ground cinnamon, ginger, cloves, nutmeg

Basic Refrigerator Items:
Soy margarine
Soymilk
Ketchup
Mustard
Grapeseed Oil Vegenaise
Water-packed tofu
Bottled lemon juice
Bragg Liquid Aminos
Vegan Worcestershire sauce
Apples, oranges, and—yes—onions!

Basic Freezer Items:
Pecans, almonds, walnuts
Apple and orange juice concentrates
Vegetables and fruits
Vegetarian meat substitutes

GROCERY LISTS

Place an ongoing grocery list in a convenient place in your kitchen and add items as they need to be replenished. (Be sure and take it with you while grocery shopping.)

FRUITS AND VEGETABLES

Only purchase fresh fruits and vegetables that will be used within 2 to 3 days. (Kept longer than that they lose not only freshness and taste but nutritional benefits as well.)

Fruit Facts: Bananas, apricots, cantaloupe, kiwi, nectarines, peaches, pears, plantains, and plums continue to ripen after they're picked. Fruits that you should pick or buy ripe and ready-to-eat include apples, cherries, grapefruit, grapes, oranges, pineapples, strawberries, tangerines, and watermelon. To speed up the ripening of fruits such as peaches, pears, and plums, put them in a ripening bowl or in a loosely closed brown paper bag at room temperature. Plastic bags don't work for ripening.

Bananas: Keep bananas fresh a little longer by storing them in the refrigerator after they've reached the desired degree of ripeness. The outside will turn brown, but they will be delicious!

Onions: Place chopped onions in small freezer bags and store in the freezer so they are ready to use in an instant! They work best in recipes that require cooking or baking and in most cases do not need to be thawed before using! A tip to decrease the tears when peeling onions—store onions in the refrigerator!

Garlic: To mince garlic without having it stick to your knife, add a few drops of water to the garlic and then chop. The garlic sticks to the cutting board and not your knife.

Lemons: To get the most juice, roll them on the counter with the palm of your hand. This will help free the juice. If you have too many lemons and don't want them to go bad, slice them into quarters and freeze in an airtight freezer bag or freezer-safe container. You can take out a little or a lot of lemon, depending upon your needs.

Fresh Herbs: Use kitchen scissors for mincing fresh herbs. It's faster than a knife. Wash and dry fresh herbs with a salad spinner.

Fresh Ginger: To peel fresh ginger quickly, scrape with the edge of the bowl of a spoon. This will remove the peel, leaving most of the ginger for use.

COOKING TIPS

When cooking vegetables, start with the veggies that take the longest to cook and keep adding, ending up with the ones that cook the fastest. A general rule of thumb would be to start with aromatics such as onions, celery, and carrots, followed by denser options such as broccoli or cauliflower, peppers, then less dense veggies such as zucchini and mushrooms, and ending with greens such as spinach and chard. For stir-fry cooking tips see Broccoli Pepper Stir-fry on page 86.

FOOD PREP

Shorten food prep time by buying already prepped vegetables such as shredded carrots, sliced mushrooms, fresh chopped onions, shredded lettuce, washed green beans, or bagged broccoli florets, etc.

TIME-SAVING GADGETS

(In no particular order of importance): Kitchen scissors, garlic press, pastry blender, sharp knifes, miniature food processor, four-sided grater, handheld blender, cookie cutter, lemon zester, citrus juicer, heat-resistant rubber spatulas, tongs, wire whisks, measuring cups and spoons, good quality vegetable peeler, digital timer, salad spinner, colander, flexible plastic cutting board, and rolling pin. Don't forget a variety of sized stainless steel scoops—the kind where you push a lever on the handle.

LARGER TIME-SAVING KITCHEN TOOLS

Rice cooker, electric Crock-Pot, electric food processor, electric knife, and pressure cooker.

PLAN MEALS AHEAD OF TIME

Make out weekly menus and save time and money! Also make cooking time family bonding time! Include the kids when preparing food and you'll not only be making delicious recipes, but you'll be making lifelong memories! And picky eaters will usually taste what they have helped prepare.

- Nonperishable foods such as cakes and cookies can be prepared a few days in advance and will still taste good. Or they can be frozen for longer storage.

- Limit the number of foods served for each meal. Prepare most perishable foods no more than 1 day prior to a meal. One-dish meals can usually be prepared a day in advance, refrigerated, and then baked just prior to your dinner. Add 15 to 20 additional minutes for heating.

- Cut washed fruits and vegetables for salads, relish trays, and stir-fry recipes ahead of time, but only 24 hours ahead at most. Celery and carrot sticks stay crisp when covered with crushed ice and refrigerated.

- Always wash fruits and vegetables with cool running water and then cover in one-time use plastic bags or storage containers. Refrigerate as soon as possible after washing and cutting. Keep apples, pears, bananas, and peaches from turning brown by coating them with a citrus juice such as lemon, orange, or pineapple. Bananas will turn brown faster than other fruits.

- Assemble all of your ingredients before starting a recipe. Be sure to read your recipe over carefully. This will save you the frustration of starting to prepare your recipe only to discover that you are missing some important ingredients!

- Don't be in too much of a hurry. Taste will be enhanced if you allow time for foods to fully blend flavors. This can be achieved by preparing food at least 30 minutes prior to serving. (This includes not only foods served hot but cold foods as well, such as pasta and fruit salads, potato salad, salad dressings, cold soups, etc.)

LAST BUT NOT LEAST

If you are trying a new recipe for the first time, follow it exactly! This way you will know how it is suppose to taste. Make any changes the second time.

Measurements & Equivalents

3 teaspoons	=	1 tablespoon
4 tablespoons	=	1/4 cup
5 tablespoons + 1 teaspoon	=	1/3 cup
8 tablespoons	=	1/2 cup
12 tablespoons	=	3/4 cup
16 tablespoons	=	1 cup
1 tablespoon	=	1/2 fluid ounce
1 cup	=	8 fluid ounces
2 cups	=	1 pint
4 cups / 2 pints	=	1 quart
4 quarts	=	1 gallon

1 teaspoon	=	5 milliliters (mL)
1 tablespoon	=	15 milliliters
1 fluid ounce	=	30 milliliters
2 fluid ounces	=	60 milliliters
8 fluid ounces (1 cup)	=	240 milliliters
16 fluid ounces (1 pint)	=	480 milliliters
32 fluid ounces (1 quart)	=	950 milliliters
128 fluid ounces (1 gallon)	=	3.75 liters

WEIGHT
Metric equivalents rounded

1/4 ounce	7 grams
1/2 ounce	14 grams
1 ounce	28 grams
4 ounces	115 grams
8 ounces (1/2 pound)	225 grams
16 ounces (1 pound)	455 grams
32 ounces (2 pounds)	910 grams
40 ounces (2 1/4 pounds)	1 kilogram

OVEN TEMPERATURE
Celsius equivalents rounded

Farenheit	Celsius	Gas setting
275 degrees	140 degrees	Mark 1
300 degrees	150 degrees	Mark 2
325 degrees	160 degrees	Mark 3
350 degrees	180 degrees	Mark 4
375 degrees	190 degrees	Mark 5
400 degrees	200 degrees	Mark 6
425 degrees	220 degrees	Mark 7
450 degrees	230 degrees	Mark 8
475 degrees	240 degrees	Mark 9
Broil		Grill

Index

BREAKFAST & BREADS

Apple Oat Waffles 16

Banana Nut Pancakes 20

Blue Corn Cakes 18

Breakfast Potatoes.....................23

Buckwheat & Flax Pancakes 19

Cinnamon & Raisin Bread........30

Grandma's Breakfast Hash 24

Honey Corn Bread Muffins.......29

Joel's Famous Hot Cereal..........26

Maple Almond Granola.............27

Multigrain Waffles.....................14

Oatmeal Raisin Muffins 28

Picante Tofu Scramble...............25

Potato Latkes............................21

Potato Pancakes 22

Pumpkin Pecan Pancakes..........17

Sweet Potato Waffles.................15

Trail Mix 31

Vibrant Life Energy Bars 32

DESSERTS

Apricot Oatmeal Cookies 118

Banana Pecan Cupcakes 126

Bananas Sanner 134

Blackberry Tarts 122

Blueberry Almost
  Ice Cream 133

Blueberry Cheesecake.............125

Cinnamon Catie-Doodles 119

Cranapple Crisp 132

Georgia Peach Shortcake 131

Granny's Fudge 137

Key Lime Pie..........................123

Lemon Poppy Seed
  Minicakes 127

Peanut Butter Bars..................120

Piña Colada............................136

Pineapple Carrot Cake 128

Pineapple Upside-Down
  Cake 130

Pumpkin Cake 129

Pumpkin Pie Squares..............121

Sweet Potato Pie 124

Tangy Citrus Parfait 135

ENTRÉES & SIDE DISHES

Broccoli Pepper Stir-fry 86

Corn Bread Pudding 83

Creamy Potato Bake.................81

Crispy Oven Fries.....................78

Enchiladas Muy Buenas............92

Italian Countryside Secondo 89

Mama's Meatloaf 91

Mashed Potato Casserole 80

Melanzana Rotini 85

Papa's Mushroom Patties 93

Pesto Mashed Potatoes..............79

Potato Spinach Patties 94

Red Pepper Fritters...................95

Roasted Vegetable Couscous......87

Scalloped Mushroom
  Potatoes 82

Spicy Arrabbiata Sauce 84

Stuffed Peppers.........................90

Vegetable Putu-Pap...................88

Index (CONTINUED)

FAST & EASY

Barley Rice Chili 102
Chicken Ratatouille.................100
Edamame Fried Rice 107
Mexican Lasagna 114
Mushroom Florentine
    Pastries.............................111
Pasta Puttanesca 106
Pesto Pomodoro Pasta 104
Portobello Mushroom
    Penne..............................105
Safari No-Bake Beans 103
South Pacific Shish Kebabs......108
Southwestern Chili Boats 112
Stuffing Tarts.......................110
Tomato Spinach Soup 101
Vegetable Burritos 113
Vegetable Chop Suey..............109

SALADS & SANDWICHES

Almond Broccoli Salad.............44
Artichoke Salad 45
Butternut Pecan Salad 36
Gringo Meal in a Pocket...........50
Marathon Salad 39
Mexican Fiesta Salad 40
Mock Egg Salad Sandwiches......47
Open-faced BLT 52
Orange Almond Salad 37
Rainbow Vegetable Salad..........38
"Ricotta" Tomato
    Sandwiches 48
Roasted Vegetable Sandwiches...49
Strawberry Pecan Salad.............43
Tijuana Salad 46
Tomato Succotash Salad 41
Veggie Oat Burgers..................51
Waldorf Coleslaw 42

SOUPS & STEWS

Butternut Squash Soup..............56
Creamy Carrot Soup 60
Curry Black Bean Soup 63
Fiesta Rice Soup 64
Garden Fresh Veggie Soup.........65
Garden Gazpacho.....................61
Mi Casa Stew 70
Pasta Fagioli 57
Poor Man's Stew 73
Red Lentil Soup 66
Rotini Tomato Soup 67
Smokey Mountain Chili...........68
Split Pea Soup 62
Sweet Potato Stew 69
Taco Soup 58
Taj Mahal Stew 71
Tomato Bisque 59
Vegetable Stew........................72

RECIPE EXTRAS

Florentine pesto.....................104
Lemon poppy seed dressing.......37

Linda's light ranch dressing........45
Strawberry dressing 43

Teriyaki sauce 86
Tomato cream sauce 80